THE LAW OF REFLECTION

(A)LIDA FEHILY

THE LAW OF REFLECTION

First published in Australia by Alida Fehily 2016
www.alidafehily.com

copyright © Alida Fehily 2016

All Rights Reserved

Catalogue-in-Publication details available from the
National Library of Australia

ISBN: 978-0-9945239-0-7 (pbk)

This book is a work of non-fiction.

Also available as an ebook: 978-0-9945239-1-4 (ebk)

© Book layout design and typesetting by Publicious P/L
www.publicious.com.au

© illustrations and cover design by:
Olton Marketing & Communication Inc.

Published with the assistance of Publicious P/L
www.publicious.com.au

In this outstanding and very easy-to-read book, Alida takes us on a journey that shows that our lives need not be directed by blind acceptance of fate or circumstances, but through a created reality – one moulded from free will and what choices we make in life.

Alida uses real world experiences (sometimes from her own painful past) to illustrate that no matter what situation we may find ourselves in right now, or what family we are born into, or even what belief system we adhere to, we all have the ability to cast our future and make it a brighter, happier and more fulfilling one.

The Law of Reflection is all about how we can make this happen and Alida, as our chaperone guide, challenges us to reflect deeply on our lives and forces us, where appropriate, to make necessary changes.

A simple yet powerful and thought-provoking book.

– Ragaie Fahmy, Barrister and Solicitor,
Melbourne, Australia

"I highly recommend this simple yet powerful book to help your world vibrate at a higher level. *The Law of Reflection* offers you a chance to view your current situation from a unique and positive perspective. No matter what stage you're at in life, *The Law of Reflection* is insightful as it challenges beliefs and shatters limitations. Its 'lessons' can be easily applied to any area of your life, such as corporate, personal or familial."

–Fabiola, Entrepreneur
Sydney, Australia

"This is exactly the book I was looking for! Alida's *The Law of Reflection* is a perfect example of "right time, right moment". I needed this book to push me forward to the next level of happiness. And it's already working!"

– Jennifer McCarthy, Writer and Journalist
Queensland, Australia

DEDICATION

This book is dedicated to my parents Brian and Pearl Fehily who guided me to "strength" and helped facilitate the changes within me that would eventually reward my life in the fullest and most complete way.

GRATITUDE

To my children Joshua and Brooke for the ongoing support and unconditional love we share.

CONTENTS

INTRODUCTION

GREETINGS FROM YOUR
ESOTERIC CHAPERONE™

Hello, I'm Alida. I'm going to be your Esoteric Chaperone™ throughout the pages of this book. Think of me as your "tour guide" as you take a journey – the journey that is your life.

I have been using the information and methods outlined in this book for many decades now, and they have not only changed my life but they have saved my life – and allowed me to live the life of my dreams.

These concepts can do the same for you.

I'm not one of those people who was "born on third base", as they say. A difficult childhood resulting from the troubled life of my parents sent me down a dark path for the first part of my life.

By the time I had reached the end of my teens, I was ready to opt out. I was considering suicide. But when I finally reached that point of ultimate darkness, I realised that I had a choice. I was at a crossroads. One path was the easy way out – just end it all, then and there. The other was to continue living – but not continue living like I had been.

One of the events that changed my life was an intimation of something deeper. At age 17, I had a dream that one of my relatives died. I awoke to discover that this in fact had occurred at the exact moment of my dream. This person lived overseas, thousands of miles away from me, yet I was able to perceive his death just as it happened. How did I know? How could I have known?

This question brought me to begin seeking answers to what was really "out there". There was obviously more to our human ability than I had been taught – or what mainstream science appeared willing to accept.

None of my schoolteachers told me about things like ESP or precognitive dreams. That was all New Age nonsense for the weak-minded, or it was "paranormal", meaning, it was "not real". I was lead to believe that only weak-minded people believed in that stuff.

However, I knew what I had experienced was real. So I started searching. I began reading as much as I could about anything and everything associated with the topic. Unfortunately, back then there wasn't all that much to choose from in terms of books and literature. Again, most "normal" people would quickly tell me that only "weird people" were into that kind of thing. Thus, I kept my newfound interest a secret from most people. Wanting to be accepted by my peers, I found it necessary to hide that part of myself from the world.

Somehow, someway – perhaps it was a kind of miracle – I made the decision to not only live on, but to search for new meanings. I was convinced that life could be better and that by finding the life of my dreams I might just embark upon an incredible journey. Keep in mind that as a young person, I still didn't know about the power of dreams – either the spontaneous kind of dream that had informed me of the death of my relative or the greater nature of all kinds of dreams.

It wouldn't be until I reached the age of 40 that I finally understood the power of dreams and the greater nature of their reality. My path to gaining greater understanding involved a lot of twists and turns in the road, as well as a lot of falling into ditches and crawling back out along the way. But it was all part of the journey. It was all meant to be. It was all good, even the pain and frustrating detours that seemingly took me away from where I intuitively knew I wanted to go. However, those "detours", "side paths" and "wrong turns" were not really bad situations either. It was all simply part of the learning, part of the journey.

I'm happy to report that it has been an amazing journey. And now it's your turn.

What you will encounter in this book is a combination of ancient wisdom, practical advice and some mystical spirituality balanced with a dollop of grounded science. My goal is to give you some shiny new tools and point you in the right direction.

In the end, I can't tell you exactly what to do. Everyone's life journey is totally unique to themselves. However, I'm going to help you by showing you how to get rid of some of the baggage that may be weighing you down right now. I am going to focus on the uplifting and positive tools you can start using immediately – today – to make changes that will transform your life from the mundane to the magic.

Life is magical. Believe it!

You only have to accept the idea that there is magic to life for magic to start happening to you – and for you. That magic will manifest in the most amazing and unexpected ways. Part of the fun of transforming your life is to experience the incredible surprises you encounter along the way.

Once you free your mind to the possibilities afforded by "unlimited thinking", the rest of your life will transform to deliver to you the unlimited potential that is waiting for you to embrace it and live it.

Your life can be a reflection of your fondest dreams. That's the Law of Reflection. You create everything that is then reflected back to you, and it becomes real in your life. Since you are the creator, the very architect of your own reality, why not take charge right now and start designing and building exactly the kind of life you have always wanted?

You just need the courage to get started. I challenge you to start thinking big and in unlimited ways right now. What do you have to lose? It doesn't cost a cent to change your mind, to simply alter your way of thinking. Yes, it's true, the best things in life are free. Your mind is free, the way you choose to think about everything is free and this is the key to your own freedom.

All the answers you seek are inside you right now. All you have to do is start looking inward to find them. I can help you do that. What you read in these pages will be a start.

However, I can only give you a start – the rest is up to you. And that's the good news. Once you make the decision to take charge and become the Grand Designer of your own life by making conscious choices and choosing how to think in positive, unlimited and abundant ways, the Universe will do everything it can to "Reflect" what is in your own mind.

You are an unlimited being meant to live a life of joy, love, adventure, fun, excitement, serenity and abundance.

All you have to do is start thinking that way and living that way right now.

CHAPTER 1

> *"Create new realities within your life filled with unlimited possibilities"*
>
> (A) LIDA FEHHLY

THE LAW OF REFLECTION

Find a quiet moment.

Take a little time to stop and reflect.

Have a good look around yourself. What do you see? What is your life like? What are your circumstances? What is your situation? Are you happy? Miserable? Perhaps you are somewhere in between. You are happy sometimes, but at other times, not so much.

Probably the majority of people reading this right now are in the "somewhere in between" category. Your life is... well... "okay". You have your happy moments and good times, but these are punctuated by periods of gloom, depression, or just a sense that something is lacking.

Most of us experience times when everything just seems to flow in our lives and fate seems to smile upon us. At other times, we can't believe our bad luck. That's normal, right? Everyone knows that life has its ups and downs. Life is a roller coaster! Or is this really "normal"?

Whatever it is you discover about yourself, and whatever situation you find yourself in right now, you can be absolutely sure of one thing:

You created this situation – every last bit of it.

Your current life condition, in all respects and aspects, is a reflection of what you have created for yourself. You manifested all this with your own free will. Even if your life is a disaster, filled with pain, worry, depression, poverty and loneliness, you can be sure that this is what you have decided to manufacture for your life right now.

For some reason, you want things this way.

It really is very simple: Your total life situation is a reflection of your own mind, your own conscious desires, but much more likely, your massive store of unconscious and subconscious programming, desires, pleasures, fears — and your solidified belief system.

Your own mind – your consciousness, subconscious, beliefs, goals and desires — is a reality-generating machine. It reaches out into the Universe to "grab" the "raw materials" that make up the fundamental basis of reality. What you choose at every minute of the day is what you get.

What you see around you and what you experience is a reflection of what your conscious mind and unconscious or subconscious mind is generating for you.

That's the Law of Reflection.

It bears repeating because this is so important to understand: The condition your life is in right now is a reflection of you, and no one else. You have created this for yourself. This is important to know, not only intellectually, but you must also psychologically internalise it. Accept it! That's because the acceptance of this basic law of how the Universe works is your first step towards creating the life you want.

Let's take a step back for a minute. Many people reading this, especially those who are living in absolute misery, might immediately protest. They cry out:

> *"Why on Earth would I actively choose to create this mess? You've got to be kidding! I would do anything to make my life better than it is now. In fact, I struggle every day trying to do just that. Everything that can go wrong has gone wrong in my life. Yet, you're trying to tell me my life is a disaster because this is what I wanted to create for myself? Get real!"*

I don't blame anyone who may think that way. Why would anyone choose to live in a situation of pain, boredom, misery, lack of money, struggle, stress, anxiety, broken relationships, etc?

Before we start to answer this central question, let's make an interesting observation about people who find themselves in the opposite situation: They are leading wonderful lives of wealth, happiness, prosperity, good health and enriching, loving relationships. Very often, you will hear a person in this enviable situation say:

"I guess I've just been blessed. I'm lucky. Sometimes I just want to pinch myself, and ask, 'Is this really happening to me?' Sure, I've worked hard for everything I have, but sometimes I'm just amazed at how everything has worked out and come together for me."

You'll notice that, just like the person with the miserable life, the happy, prosperous person seems perplexed by the way life has turned out for them. They're rich, happy and have it all, but they credit some mysterious outside source, such as "luck", or "being blessed".

The fact is, happy and prosperous people create their life situations in every bit the same way as poor and miserable people create their life situations. It's a reflection of their own consciousness, the choices they have made of their own free will and, beyond that, the unfolding of a grand plan that these individuals have outlined for themselves for this lifetime.

True, happy and prosperous people are much more likely to take credit for their enviable situation. Why not? The ego is always ready to stand up to boast, brag and build itself up – even though your ego has nothing to do with how wealthy or poor you are. (We'll talk much more about the ego later.)

Whatever the case, it's such a common human trait: We give ourselves great credit for all our successes and we rail against the fates for all our failures. Yet, the hard fact is, even happy and successful people are often oblivious to how their reality has come to be.

WHAT'S GOING ON HERE?

Anyone who has read a New Age book, or two, or three, is probably already familiar with the following claim: "You create your own reality."

I know, I know, a lot of us hear this so often today that it has almost become a cliché. The idea that we all create our own reality is a powerful concept but today there are so many books, gurus, self-help success seminar leaders and New Agers out there pushing and 'selling' this idea. It's almost as if this most fundamental tenet of our lives has lost some if its punch.

When the truth becomes a fad, it starts to feel watered down. People become fatigued with hearing the same old thing from so many voices. Many of those speakers only seem to be telling us what we want to hear so they can make money writing books or giving seminars.

But the fact is, the concept that we create our own reality is not only true — ***it is ancient.***

It is a universal truth that has withstood not just centuries of time, but thousands of years. The truth that we create our own reality is fundamental. You might even say that it is "The First Law". It is from this that the rest of our lives flow.

SCIENCE SUPPORTS THE LAW OF REFLECTION

To help convince you that the Law of Reflection is real and that every human being truly does create his or her own reality, the next few pages may be a bit of hard work for some of you – even perhaps a tad dull or boring. Skim it or skip it if you want.

If you need some extra convincing that what I will be talking about in the rest of the this book is completely real, totally sound and based on actual historic fact and science, it will be enormously helpful to take a closer look at how we came to be where we are today: A species that is actually waking up to a new reality. This 'new' reality is actually as ancient as humankind itself, but it seems new to us now because of what has been forgotten over the past 500 years.

ANCIENT WISDOM COMES FULL CIRCLE

What's fascinating about the concept that we create our own reality is we find evidence for this idea in some of the Earth's most ancient writings and cultures. The idea has persisted throughout the long march of time. The concept that we create our own reality has never really gone away – but in recent centuries, it has become 'hidden'. This happened for a specific reason, and it all began about 500 years ago.

As a point of reference, we can fairly point to the Polish Renaissance astronomer, Nicolaus Copernicus (1473–1543), who came out with his sun-centred theory – then our entire 'world view' began to change. That was just a little more than 500 years ago. After Copernicus' discovery, the community of all of Earth's people – of all religions, persuasions and cultures – began to change, and they did so by turning away from the ancient beliefs of the past.

Prior to Copernicus's discovery, the vast bulk of the world's population framed their world in terms of religious beliefs, spiritual notions and supernatural explanations. A more general term often used to describe the pre-scientific/technological age is "Hermeticism". Under Hermeticism, ultimate reality is understood to be variously God, the All, or the One. This "Ultimate Source" was seen as unitary and transcendent.

While there is much to be said for Hermeticism, there is no denying that from a modern point of view a lot of things just didn't add up under a Hermetic system. For example, before Copernicus, some five centuries ago, the general belief was that the Earth was flat. The Earth was the centre of the Universe, and the Sun, other planets and all the stars revolved around the Earth.

Everyone thought it was true because they believed that was what the Bible informed them about the formation of the heavens. Even before the Old Testament was written and among other faiths outside Christianity, including pagan beliefs, all philosophies placed Earth at the centre of everything created by the "Almighty One", God or "All That Is". Of course, much depended on the way certain passages of the Bible and other sacred texts were interpreted – but it also seemed an article of common sense.

After all, when you go out and stand in a flat field, the Earth does not look round. Standing in an open plain or in the middle of a vast desert, the Earth seems to stretch out flat as a pancake in all directions as far as the eye can see. It seems just common sense that the Earth is flat because it looks flat and feels flat. Also, if the Earth was round, why didn't things just roll off the surface? Again, this seems like a powerful article of plain old common sense.

It also seemed the most basic common sense that the Sun was revolving or circling around the "Flat Table" of the Earth while the Earth stood still. It was easy to see the Sun come up in the east and go down in the west. It was the Sun that appeared to be moving across the sky. That the opposite was true seemed completely ridiculous 500 years ago. After all, if it was the Earth that was moving around the Sun, then how come people didn't *feel* anything moving? If the Earth was flying through space, why does the ground seem so solid and stable beneath our feet? If it was moving, where was the sense of motion, or even perhaps a passing breeze?

Then came Copernicus. Armed with hard mathematics and direct observational science, he proved that everything we thought we knew about the cosmos was wrong. The Earth was not the centre of the solar system – rather, the Sun. The Sun did not revolve around the Earth. Just the opposite was true! Not only did the Earth revolve around the Sun but the Earth was not flat, but round. Not only was the Earth round and flying around the Sun but it was also revolving on its axis at a rapid rate. To the common person of 500 years ago, this seemed not just ridiculous but absolutely beyond ridiculous and certainly impossible.

The fact is that most people today are just as naïve about many aspects of our reality, and how it all works in our world, as the people of the pre-Copernican world. We think we are living in a scientific society that has all the answers. But are we? The idea of accepting the fact we create our own reality is a prime case in point. Just as people 500 years ago doubted a round, orbiting Earth, people today are asking:

"How is it possible that I can create my own reality? I'm just an ordinary biological human being. I'm not a reality-generating machine!"

"If I am creating my own reality, why have I made such a mess of my personal life – and why is the rest of the world such a dangerous and sad place, too?"

"How can I be creating my reality when there are people all around me? Whose reality am I in, my own or everyone else's?"

Some pretty vexing questions, to be sure.

Just as people 500 years ago found it impossible to believe the Earth could be round and spinning, so today many people cannot accept or grasp the concept we create our own reality. How could it be possible? Once again, it seems to defy common sense. But remember how wrong our "common sense" was 500 years ago?

Before I address all of these kinds of questions, I want to finish my point about Copernicus and the scientific revolution that he ushered in. After Copernicus was eventually proven to be correct, it seemed that the hard sciences, and only the hard sciences, had all the answers.

Other brilliant thinkers followed Copernicus and they continued to reshape the way humanity thought about the world.

The true giant of history who was perhaps most responsible for the materialistic, hard science-oriented trap we find ourselves in today was Isaac Newton. A genius of monumental proportions, the gist of Newton's science had the effect of declaring "all matter dead". He created what we call "the billiard ball Universe". Newton proclaimed that all of reality is made up of fundamental building blocks – atoms – and these are the smallest solid bits of reality.

Everything was made up of atoms (the tiniest billiard balls) – including people. On a fundamental level, everything is "dead". But when you add energy to atoms, they can be prompted into motion and start "acting like" living things. Sure, everything is moving around and interacting, but all of this is largely an illusion in the Newtonian worldview. Once any system runs out of energy, it goes back to being "dead". It is as if it were never alive in the first place.

That includes the human body and mind. Stop inputting energy into it (food and water) and see how quickly a body stops acting alive and starts 'acting' dead! Maybe the body was never truly alive in the first place. Maybe it was all just some kind of grand illusion.

Newton is famous for envisioning the Universe as a gigantic clock, the famous "Clockwork Universe". He suggested that somewhere back in the unimaginably distant reaches of time, God wound up the clock, set it in motion, then more or less disappeared from the scene. As long as there is still some tension and thus energy in the "clock springs of the Universe", everything will keep running – but eventually it will all run out – and the Universe will die of entropy.

Newton was never much about answering the "Why?" questions. He just endeavoured to explain *"how"* things are. Why would God wind up the Big Clock then more or less vanish from the scene, leaving humanity to fend for itself? Newton just shrugged his mighty shoulders and said: *"That's not for me to say."*

Why have I taken the time to provide this short lesson on the history of science? It's a risk, I know, because many people are quickly bored with that kind of subject matter. However, I wanted to help you all see how you, me and all of humanity has gotten ourselves into so much trouble lately – and how we have managed to forget the most fundamental law of our lives – we create our own reality.

You see, after Newton, the hard, material-science worldview took over almost our entire planet. It became embedded in the minds of all people. Anything that could not be proven with maths, numbers and physical experiments is quickly disregarded as "mysticism" at best, and "New Age Voodoo" at worst.

That's how centuries and millennia of our most ancient and truthful wisdoms were pushed to the sidelines, marginalised and largely tossed into the cultural trash can.

"We create our own reality?" Ridiculous! Show me the proof! What mathematical formula defines that? Sigmund Freud called that "wishful thinking". What scientific models or natural laws support the idea that we create our own reality? If it's true, why are so many people suffering and miserable? Preposterous!

"If wishes were fishes, we'd all cast our nets!"

"Show me the money!"

SCIENCE HAS COME FULL CIRCLE

Just as it was hard, materialistic science that pushed aside the idea that we create our own reality, it is now that same science that has not only brought back the idea but provided a solid, scientific foundation that literally proves that each human being is in control of every facet of his or her personal existence. Each and every aspect of your life is something you create moment-to-moment, second-to-second, instant-to-instant.

Actually, it is a new brand of science that supports this view: quantum mechanics.

The old regime of physics is referred to as Newtonian Physics. The new system is quantum mechanics, or quantum theory.

No, don't worry. I'm not going to launch into a dry, technical lecture on how quantum theory works. Rather, I think it is important for you to know the most basic fundamentals of how this New Science supports the ancient wisdom of our millennia-old past, when spiritual ideas and so-called "supernatural" forces were accepted as fact.

The word supernatural is just a word we apply to things that science does not yet understand.

It is important you understand that today's most solid, accepted and mainstream science supports the idea that we create our own reality. It is important for shaping, or reshaping, your fundamental belief system.

Right now, the vast majority of people reading this – whether they know it or not – still hold onto a deep-seated doubt that The Law of Reflection is reality, and doubt that we do in fact create our own reality and world situation. Until you dig down deep and root out all disbelief and resistance to the idea that you can attract whatever you want in life, your ability to do so will be limited.

The resistance comes from the science you have been inundated with throughout your entire life. Even if you never paid attention in school when it came to your science lessons and don't know or care to know anything about science, the fact is you are steeped in what is generally believed scientifically by the culture all around you and in which you were raised.

You almost certainly have come to believe that unless the accepted mainstream scientific community pronounces something "true", or "untrue", everything else you believe becomes secondary.

While there are thousands of books available today about the laws of attracting wealth, peace and harmony into your life – and tens of thousands of people have attested to the fact that it works – we also hear just as often the scornful denouncements from the so-called scientific community and "the sceptics".

We hear:

> *"It's amazing how gullible people are. Some New Age guru tells them that they can create anything they want in life with their own minds, and people line up to buy this latest version of hocus-pocus snake oil."*

But the so-called "sceptics" are not really sceptics at all. They are true believers. Just as those religious fundamentalists who believe their particular version of their chosen faith is the one and only correct belief system, those who believe in the ultimate authority of science have fallen into the same trap. Little do they realise that the science in which they put their stock has long since been rendered obsolete by more advanced scientific models.

The Newtonian world of "matter is dead" and a pre-destined "Clockwork Universe" has long since been overturned by the new science of quantum mechanics. quantum mechanics informs us that:

- All matter is not dead. All matter is alive at its most fundamental level.

- There is no solid matter, no "billiard balls", no basic building blocks of the Universe.

- Everything is made up of energy.

- The atoms that compose our bodies are 99.99999% empty space.

- The "stuff" the human body is made up of is also 99.999999% empty space.

- The human body is basically a jittering, glowing cloud of energy acting as matter.

- Consciousness is not generated by the human brain; rather, the brain only "tunes in" the consciousness that is being transmitted from 'out there'.

- All consciousness is non-local. (Not centred in the human brain).

- Consciousness is basically made up of pure energy.

- All 'physical matter reality', including our own human bodies, the Earth and our environment and everything in it, is made from pure consciousness.

Most scientists today will be the first to tell you that they accept all the precepts and implications of quantum mechanics, but they are stuck 'acting like' and 'believing' we are still operating in the old Newtonian System. Generally, they say that the quantum rules apply only to the tiny subatomic world but the rest of the 'Big World', which we all live our lives within, is still a Newtonian World.

But they are wrong.

The rules of quantum world are the rules that make up our daily lives, or 'Big Lives', our natural environment, and everything we experience in our daily lives and the world around us. This means we are not physical beings – we are spiritual beings made up of pure energy. The solid, physical bodies we associate with so closely are not our real selves. In fact, the concept that our physical bodies are "who we are" is a kind of persistent delusion.

The reality is, we are projecting our minds into our physical bodies from an outside location. Think of the physical world we live in as a virtual reality world in the same way that a computer video game is a virtual reality world.

When you play a video game, you have an avatar on the screen that you control with a joystick, or the buttons on your play module. Your avatar might be a magic elf, a knight in shining armour who is battling video dragons, or a soldier playing "shoot it up" with swarms of enemies. (Unfortunately, many video games are based around violence.)

But who is actually controlling the little soldier, knight or elf on the computer screen? The player! That's you! When you press a button, the avatar runs to the left. Press the opposite button and it scuttles to the right. Press "jump" and it jumps! You are controlling its every move and action from outside the computer itself.

This is similar to the way your real life is happening right now. Your physical body is the "avatar" and your "spirit", "soul" or "consciousness" is the game controller, pressing the buttons and giving commands to what is happening here in your physical matter reality.

This is why the Law of Attraction is real, and why the Law of Attraction works. It is because your true mind, your consciousness, is actually outside of what you perceive as your physical world. As your mind is exterior and therefore in control, you can take direct action to shape the environment around you. You can cause things to come into your life and you can command other things to get out of your life.

Things don't just 'happen' to you. The fact is you are directing all the action from an outside source. Most people don't know that this is the way it works. Once again, because of the old scientific models you have adopted and become trapped within, you've come to believe you are "victims" of whatever your environment or circumstances dishes out. It is time for everyone to come to grips with the fact that this is wrong. The environment does not shape us – we shape it. The science of quantum mechanics proves that this is the case. It is important you believe that this is true – because it is!

I can't express this enough: For the Law of Reflection and the Law of Attraction to truly work for you, **you must believe it really can work for you.** You may or may not need more convincing. After all, millions of people have already discovered that this process truly does work; you can create the life of your dreams and attract your heart's desires into your life by focusing your thoughts and feeling your feelings with the right intentions.

TRANSFORMING YOUR BELIEF SYSTEM

You are where you are right now because of the belief system you accept and hold in your mind every day. I'm not saying this is a bad thing. All of us are where we are supposed to be. This does not mean you have to like the situation you are in right now. You are exactly where you are supposed to be, but there is nothing that says you can't make changes to your life.

Change starts with recognising that it is your belief system that is generating your reality. I could spend a lot of time explaining exactly what a belief system is but let's simplify it by saying your belief system is made up of *the various assumptions you hold about your reality.*

Interestingly, you will also experience many "proofs" every day of what you believe about reality. For example, it may be your firm belief that the only way to get ahead in life is to *"work very hard and work long hours each day"*. This is a very common belief system.

People who believe this look around and see "proofs" of it all the time. They notice other people who are "working very hard" and they seem to be getting ahead and have most of what they want in life. They may also notice that as long as they themselves are working hard, they tend to keep the bills paid and have enough money for all the basic things they require. They also seem to notice that if they stop working, suddenly they are short of money, bills start piling up, and so on.

Is it really true? Is having everything you want in life obtained by *"working very hard"?*

The fact is it's not true. The proof that everyone must "work very hard" is blown apart by the obvious fact that there are all kinds of people not working hard, or not even working at all, who still have everything they want in life. You may even know such people personally.

Some people are just born rich, so they don't have to work. Other people do what they love – such as an artist creating landscape paintings, or an inventor tinkering together amazing devices – but they work only when they want to, or feel inspired to work.

If they don't want to "work hard", they don't; if they do want to "work hard", they do.

Yet, the landscape painter may make enough money from selling just one or two paintings per year to enjoy a fabulous lifestyle of wealth. The inventor might strike it rich with just one creation, and never have to work again.

The point is, the idea that "all people have to work hard" to get ahead in life is **not a fundamental truth.** It is very clear that it is not a fundamental truth because it does not apply to everyone.

The idea that *"You must work hard to get ahead"* is nothing more than a belief system. If it is your belief system, then don't be surprised that the only way you seem able to get by is by always *"working hard".*

That's what you are creating for yourself through your belief system because you hold, nurture and maintain this mental, thought-based system.

What if you changed your belief system? Let's say that one day you just decide that getting everything you want out of life is:

"Easy, fun, enjoyable and doesn't involve any work that is not pleasant for Me."

What if you adopted this belief system and thoroughly convinced yourself that it was 100% true? Would your life then become **easy, fun and enjoyable, filled with pleasant work?**

Yes, it would!

If you find this *"hard to believe"*, that's because it seems to violate the basic rules of your current belief system.

The fact is, your life can transform from a *"hard work only"* belief system to an *"easy, fun, light and pleasant work only"* belief system because this is one of the most fundamental laws of your very existence — that your reality is formed by your belief system.

If this sounds just too good to be true, then all you need to do is start testing the theory in your own life. After you successfully attract or magnetise something into your life you really want — and discover how easy it is — you will soon begin to accept this process is true. You will have your "proof".

MONEY IS DANGEROUS?

Now just to drive my point home, let's look at another common belief: that there is something wrong with having large amounts of money.

Most people wish every day they had a huge amount of money, so much so they would never have to worry about money again. And yet, they find that getting a large amount of money seems to be absolutely impossible.

Why?

Again, this situation is rooted in their belief systems.

First of all, there are many forces and sources of philosophy in our society that glorify poverty, or at least a state of having very little money. Most of the major mainstream religions hold up "the poor" as being the most innocent, decent and humble people. They provide us with images of saints who became, well, "saintly", by catering to the poor, while also living among and like the poor themselves.

Just about all the major religious texts contain stories of how poor people tend to be the most spiritual and stand the best chance of getting into Heaven.

However, there are also other sources in our daily lives that seem to "prove" to us that having large amounts of money is dangerous. For example, just about every day we hear something in the media about a famous rich person who is in some kind of trouble.

Some movie stars always seem to be getting divorced or addicted to drugs. Other fabulously wealthy celebrities commit suicide. Still others profess to be living lives of depression and unhappiness, despite being amazingly rich and famous.

How many times have you heard about a child movie star who had his or her life ruined by too much "early fame and wealth"? Or every so often we see a story about a lottery winner who had his or her life destroyed by obtaining too much sudden wealth.

We also see, hear or read daily stories about people who became extremely rich through corrupt means such as cheating others on complicated pyramid schemes, banking fraud or "breaking the rules" in hundreds of different ways. A lot of people think "you have to be crooked" to get rich. Or they think you have to be greedy and ready to "step on others" to gain a lot of money.

The point is, many people harbour deep-seated fears, doubts and mistrust about having a lot of money. It's part of their belief system. They think owning a large sum of money will be a burden or they fear that it will cause others to "love them only for their money". The fact is, people can come up with a million reasons why they should avoid getting rich, whether they know it or not.

However, it's all purely a matter of belief. The reality is every single negative belief you can think of about having a lot of money is a matter of belief, not a matter of solid reality. The fact is, you can adopt any kind of belief you want about money, including the belief that having all the money you want is perfectly fine and good. You can even believe that having a lot of money doesn't mean you're any less spiritual.

In a coming chapter I'll be talking about the value of making a searching and thorough self-examination of your own belief system, including rethinking your most fundamental beliefs about money.

The point I want to make for now is that once you identify any negative or limiting beliefs you have about money, you can learn to turn your attention away from them and start to formulate new beliefs that are more in line with the life of your dreams.

YOU DESERVE IT

If you don't like the life you are living right now, you deserve to live a different kind of life, one that is in line with your deepest desires. You deserve to be doing something that makes your heart sing, while also providing all the basic elements of a free, happy and independent lifestyle.

Let me ask you this: "Can you think of a reason why you shouldn't have everything you want and be living the life you want?"

Let me also ask you:

"Do you really believe you deserve to enjoy the life of your dreams?"

In my work, I have been constantly surprised by how quickly many people responded negatively to these two questions. When these questions were put to them, they have listed things about themselves or their pasts that they believed were stopping them from achieving – or even striving for – their heartfelt desires and goals. Every person is carrying some kind of guilt, plus they are often riddled with doubts about their own powers and abilities.

One person to whom I posed these questions answered:

"I was a horrible bully all through my school years, and no one ever called me out on it. I guess I just got away with it. I had everyone afraid of me, and that's the way I wanted it. As I grew older, I came to regret my youthful behaviour; in fact, I'm deeply ashamed of the kind of person I used to be. So I think I have to spend the rest of my life making amends and learning to live with a certain amount of suffering."

This is a classic example of a person nurturing guilt. Notice he has since changed his life and no longer bullies, and even feels sorrow and regret. He even took steps to make amends to some of his former classmates – and yet, he still feels he does not deserve to live the life of his dreams because of his past mistakes.

The reality is that it is time for him to move on. He now deserves to lead a wonderful life full of abundance and joy which involves giving to and helping others. For this man to live in poverty for the rest of his life makes no sense. The point is: It is important to ask yourself what might be holding you back based on what you think you deserve and don't deserve.

Another example:

A woman told me she is not smart enough to quit her boring, soul-killing, low-paying job because she simply isn't clever enough to start her own business, even though that has long been her secret desire.

She feels she **does not deserve** a better life simply because she is not intelligent. She has adopted a personal belief system that has convinced her that she naturally lacks intelligence, and therefore is stuck with that condition for the rest of her life.

The truth is that lack of intelligence has not prevented thousands, if not millions of people from living the life of their dreams. Many people have identified areas where they lack knowledge and have taken action to change that situation.

Some of them take night courses at a local college or embark upon further education. Others go to a library and read every book they can about a particular subject they want to learn more about. Still others just plunge ahead and learn from life itself just by "doing". However, none of the above can happen as long as a person remains trapped in a belief system that tells them they have a particular limitation such as intelligence.

Take it from me personally: Some of the least intelligent people I know are the richest and happiest. I don't say that in an insulting way. I say it simply because it is true. In fact, there is nothing particularly wrong with you if you're not an intellectual. You don't have to be the sharpest tool in the shed to be happy.

Our society puts way too much emphasis on intellect. There are tonnes of people who command very powerful intellectual gifts who are living lives of misery.

What really matters is your "state of beingness". Human beings are more than just intellect. We are made up of a variety of "states", such as emotional patterns, a sense of kindness and justice, a capacity to do what is right, along with ambitions to pursue interesting and important roles. In the end, it's all about heart and intention. Life is a journey for all of us, and we've all been granted a certain amount of gifts and traits in varying degrees. There is no one perfect "magic formula" that equates to one's ability to live exactly the kind of life one wants to live.

If you sense something lacking in your life right now, what new belief or attitude could you adopt to remedy the situation? Are you able to visualise an image that shows you a way in which you are allowed to have what you really want? Ask yourself: "What do I deserve?" Then, when old cobwebs surface that seem to tell you why you "don't deserve" what you want, start eliminating them, one by one. Instead, focus on what you "do deserve"; look at the positive rather than the negative.

Try to eliminate any excuse you have for "not deserving" anything for the very simple reason that all of these excuses are false. These false excuses are based on nothing more than artificial beliefs which you can change or discard at any time.

SUMMARY AND ACTION POINTS

- You create your own reality. Everything you see around you, for better or worse, is something you have created for yourself.

- Your own mind/consciousness is the "machine" that generates your reality.

- Most people are not aware that they are creating their own reality, and thus, don't understand how they end up in their current life situation.

- Cutting-edge science supports the idea that we create our own reality.

- Mainstream science (the old science) is still sceptical (and mostly rejects) the idea that we create our own reality – and this causes most people to doubt the proposition that in fact we have total control over our own lives and situations.

- It's important to understand we are struggling as a society to overturn the old paradigm of materialistic science and replace it with science that acknowledges the power of the purely non-physical and spiritual – the pure realm of the mind and consciousness.

- The Law of Reflection bears out this new reality – and explains your world. When you understand you create your own reality, and come to accept this concept, you take the first step towards authentic power. This is because once you realise you can create your own reality you can start actively creating the reality you want for yourself. Then, rather than allowing things to happen at random, or as the result of unintentionally holding onto repetitive negative ideas, you can twirl your magic wand, so to speak, and conjure up your fairy tale life in your current reality.

- You deserve to have everything you want.

- You deserve to live the life of your dreams.

Now that you understand that you create your own reality, and that both science and ancient spiritual traditions support this genuine reality, you are ready to take the first steps to change your life and start living the life of your dreams.

CHAPTER 2

> *"Listen to the wisdom of your soul,*
> *it knows its purpose"*
>
> (A)LIDA FEHILY

YOUR LIFE PURPOSE: PRE-ENCODED, BUT WITH FREE WILL TO CHOOSE AND CHANGE

One of the questions I am asked most often is:

"Do we have a pre-encoded life purpose?"

It's an interesting question. It points to a lot of the central issues that are important to understand if you are going to finally gain control of your life and start creating the kind of life you want for yourself.

Without a doubt we are born into lives and an existence that, in large part, is pre-encoded. Think of all the attributes that are encoded and determined by our DNA, for example. We have certain archetypes we play out in life. One might also point to astrology and how it shows that there are broad, pre-set categories that people fit into; an Aries will tend to have a lot of the same traits as another Aries and a Libran will share many similarities with others of that sign.

If you don't believe in astrology, then I would point to those archetypes I mentioned. The idea that all human beings engender certain archetypical traits was championed by the great Swiss psychologist Carl Jung. His ideas (broadly accepted by the scientific community) are highly similar to what is suggested by astrology. There are broad categories of traits that groups of people adopt, share and play out within their lives.

The point is it's obvious that so much about our lives is pre-programmed for us. It's all set and ready to go the day we are born. When we come out of the womb and into the world, our "programs" are set in motion.

We're off and running at the game of life.

We're playing by a broad set of pre-determined rules and pre-programmed codes – and we agreed to adopt these rules and codes before we were born into this reality.

Thus, so much of what you are is already there from the day you're born. These pre-encoded aspects that make up yourself will have a large effect on who and what you are, and how your life will play out.

It might be helpful to understand and visualise this if we compare it to a computer video game.

In a video game, we have what is called a pre-encoded "rule set". A character in a video game, for example, will have all his or her traits pre-programmed by the code writer who created the computer game. The code writer gives the video game character a set of traits and characteristics, then he or she creates the "rule set" for the environment he or she will play the game in.

The video game character might be an elf with green skin, pointy ears and large, almond-shaped eyes. Maybe he has magical powers that allow him to jump 100 feet into the air and shoot fire bolts out of his fingertips. Those are "natural abilities" he inherits from birth because they are pre-encoded into him.

His environment might be an enchanted land of castles, dragons and goblins, which he must fight to defeat in order to achieve his goal. Perhaps his challenge is to capture a golden cup, or rescue the Elf Princess. That's his pre-encoded existence and role in his "life".

As human beings, we are in much the same situation. Yes, our reality is much more complex than a simple computer video game, but the comparison is interesting and helpful to make.

A big difference, however, is that the computer-game elf does not have free will. We do.

Even so, like the computer elf (or avatar) we come into our world environment with the "codes" that God, Mother Nature, genetics or whatever you want to call it, gave us. Also, like the video game character, we operate in an environment with a certain "rule set".

Our rule set is the basic laws of nature. For example, we have gravity, which means that, unlike our elf, we can't jump 100 feet into the air. We can jump only a couple of feet off the ground – unless you're an Olympic athlete, perhaps, but even an Olympic athlete is ultimately limited by gravity.

If we go outside without a coat, head covering, gloves and insulated boots and it's 20-below-zero outside, we would freeze to death. The rule set of Mother Nature says your human body can only operate comfortably within a certain temperature range. The rule set also says your body needs to be supplied with food and water periodically – or else it will run out of energy and die. This pre-determined rule set is the one we must obey – we have no choice.

However, obeying the "rule set" of our natural environment doesn't mean we are robots (or characters in a computer game). That's because, as I mentioned previously, we also have free will. Yes, we have to obey certain rules and constraints, but not only do we have free will, we also possess a far greater ability to shape the world we live in according to the way we want it to be.

There are some areas that are pre-encoded and that we can't change like the law of gravity, the temperature outside or the amount of oxygen in the atmosphere. We also can't change our fundamental physical characteristics. For example, I'm 5-feet tall, so no matter how much I wish upon a star, I won't grow any taller. That's the bottom line, so that's an example of something that is pre-encoded and set for life.

Sure, some people can do a lot to alter their physical appearance in other ways. For example, a body builder can pump iron for five hours a day to transform his "98-pound weakling" body into a powerful muscle-bound hulk. A person who is obese and weighs 400 pounds can go on a strict diet, adopt a rigorous exercise program, and transform him or herself into a sleek 160-pound picture of perfect health. But even dramatic alterations like these are only surface-level changes. We can't change the fundamentals.

So again, these pre-encoded aspects I'm talking about are things like your height, your eye colour, skin colour, blood type, the shape of your head, face and other features. Yes, you might alter some of these things with extraordinary effort – after all, you can go to a plastic surgeon and have a nose job! But your genetics ultimately determine the shape and type of body you have; even a plastic surgeon can only do so much to change the way you look. You inherit the physical body you have from your parents, your grandparents and other ancestors. You come from a specific genetic pool and this determines so much about you.

The fact is there are more than 4,600 inherited human traits. Consider that. That's a lot of traits! They're all pre-encoded, set in stone (or in this case, set in flesh), aspects of our reality that we cannot alter. It's what we have to work with. It's all within us.

Biological families share the same biological pools. So when you are born into a family, your different roles and personalities will play out, partially dictated by the traits you've inherit along with the traits inherited by your other family members. Many diseases, for example, run in families. Some families have a lot of members who are diabetic, or suffer arthritis. Others have weak hearts or are highly prone to migraine headaches. We have all observed this. It's "in the family", as we say.

It should also be mentioned that not all inherited family traits are negative. Some families are gifted with wonderful traits such as beautiful faces, bodies and naturally athletic abilities. Other families have the gift of genius running through them. A classic example is the Huxley family. Aldous Huxley was famous for writing the groundbreaking novel, Brave New World. He was also known to have a genius-level IQ. His three brothers Julian, Andrew and David were all brilliant in their own fields. Their grandfather, Thomas Huxley, was a major figure in the then cutting-edge science of evolution and who was on par with giants of history such as Charles Darwin.

It's all part of the grand design of that family. Your family has a design, too. You may not be a member of a genius family, or a disease-ridden family, but your family still has a special design of its own.

Not only do we have inherited family traits, we also have inherited patterns of belief systems. Family members bring thoughts and belief patterns along with them down through the generations and each family member resonates with those particular thoughts and beliefs. Remember, it's only a thought or belief and you have the power to change it at will.

All of these traits, physical traits and belief system traits, create a certain family dynamic which is part of the drama we have been born to play out and participate in. Some families are seen as highly dysfunctional. I can attest to that since I myself came from a family plagued by abuse and violence – but there is always a purpose to these kinds of dysfunctional natures.

In a broader sense, there really is no "dysfunction". That's because each family is designed to be what it is – and that allows us to play out the roles we were destined to take on in this lifetime. We accept these conditions in prior-birth "contracts" so that we can have certain experiences. It's from these experiences that we are given challenges to face and these have the effect of forcing us into situations in which we grow spiritually.

The wonderful thing is that, no matter what kind of family and belief system we are born into, we have a great deal of power to change it. We can radically alter negative, "dysfunctional" belief systems and dynamics within familial situations. The fact that you were born into an abusive family does not mean you cannot change it, escape from it, or even leverage the dark times you experience to see more light. The purpose of those dark and challenging times is to make you find a way to grow and become even happier and more fulfilled than you otherwise might have been.

When you look at each and every one of us, all of us have chosen to come to the physical earth plane with a designed destiny. However, we have many different pathways and possibilities to lead us forward. The fact that there are many pathways – or choices – that lead us into the future is highly significant. So much of your past may appear to be set in stone by inherited traits and family systems you were born into, but the future is really wide open. The future is open for you to mould and shape because you make choices every day. Every time you make a choice, you are taken down a certain pathway into the future.

When we begin to understand and realise that the choices made today shape and determine our future, we can then start being more careful and thoughtful about the choices we make. We can begin to make choices that take us where we truly want to go, rather than being controlled by random events, or the programming of our past.

We start to become actors in our lives, rather than reactors.

The fact that there are multiple pathways into the future means you will go down roads that introduce you to different people depending on what choices you are making. If you go down one pathway, you're going to meet Joe, but if you make a different choice, you are sent down another pathway, where you might meet Mary instead.

So, when you think about it, the people who come into our lives and who are important to us are the results of choices we make every day. In fact, all of the people we meet and interact with in our lives have some vital purpose or meaning to us. Even people we meet briefly serve some purpose.

If you are a single person, the choices you make today may launch you on a path that will lead directly to your future wife or husband. You might also meet the person who will provide you with your dream job, or who will become the perfect business partner.

Yes, your choices might also lead to people who have a not-so-positive influence in your life. Who among us has not had a disastrous relationship? Sometimes we meet a person we thought we were in love with, only to discover later that this individual was probably the last person on the planet we should have hooked up with. Who among us hasn't had an opportunity to ponder: "My God! What was I thinking when I hooked up with Bob (or Jane, or Sam, or Margaret)?"

It sure seemed like a good idea at the time!

Yes, there are choices that lead us to positive, growing and enriching relationships, and those which – well, let's just say, might teach us some very challenging lessons in life. It can all seem pretty overwhelming. I use the term "challenging" rather than "painful" when I talk about life experiences. That's because there truly are no "painful" experiences. It all depends on how we choose to view such events.

Everyone we meet, for good or ill, is part of the experience we are having in this lifetime. Our human experience is to have an extraordinary journey in life that fulfills our existence and interacts with our spiritual connection with Oneness.

It is our free will to make choices. How we make those choices determines how we follow our purpose. It determines whether we discover our true purpose, or go astray. Our free will choices determine whether or not we fulfill the destiny that matches our fondest dreams, or if we will stay mired in a place of helplessness, feeling 'victimised' by life and our individual circumstances.

Again, let me use myself as an example. The family I perceived I came from was a family of violence. I was subjected to so much emotional and physical abuse that, even by the age of five, I was already contemplating ending my own life by suicide. I would later actually try to carry out my plans to kill myself. I also went down some others paths based on negative choices such as "smoking weed" and turning to other "fixes" that weren't really fixes at all. I did so to hide what I perceived to be emotional pain at the time.

Of course, this "emotional" pain was actually a valuable experience but at the time the family experiences I encountered seemed to be showing me that "life is hell". At the time, I believed that as human beings, we must be thrust into horrible situations seemingly at random, or by a cruel God. The family I was born into seemed like proof in my mind that there was something wrong with me, that I wasn't good enough and that I would never amount to anything.

I could have continued to go down a destructive path of drugs and suicide attempts but everything that was happening to me within my own family ultimately caused me go further, to seek answers, and to ask poignant questions of myself:

"Who am I?"

"What is this all about?"

"Was I just put on this Earth to suffer and be abused?"

"What is wrong with me?"

"Do I deserve all of this, or am I an innocent victim?"

"Do I have to accept my fate?"

It was tough questions like these that pushed me to go beyond what my mind was showing me – what my life-experiences were delivering to me – and turn to the depths of my soul to seek answers.

As difficult as a dysfunctional family can be, the situation can also be looked upon as a gift that forces us to look within. We can search and search and search for answers to our negative life situation in locations "out there" – outside of ourselves – but as is suggested in numerous ancient texts: "The answers lie within."

When I started to listen to the love and wisdom that is naturally within myself, rather than what the perceptions of my mind seemed to be showing me in terms of my outward life situation, I was amazed to find that my true life purpose was actually there – and more evident.

It became clear to me that we have all the answers we need within ourselves on a deeper level. My purpose, our purpose, your purpose has and always has been right there inside you, as close as your own breath. It is ready to manifest itself according to the thoughts you choose to hold on to on a daily basis. It is the thought-forms you select to dominate your mind, which you keep front and centre, that will most shape how your life and reality unfold from day to day.

If you are immersed within and surrounded by darkness and negativity – as I was in my family life – it is difficult not to accept your experiences as common sense, 'feedback' of 'just the way things are'. But that is a choice. You only choose to accept the situation you are in as "inevitable" and a "reality" because you seem to be stuck there. It seems as if you are "really there".

While there may appear to be many hurdles to gaining true happiness, the only things stopping you from simply changing your situation is yourself and your entrenched beliefs. If you start to look at all aspects of your life in a different way, you can start to make different choices using your natural gift of free will.

You can also stop looking for all of the answers "out there", and turn inward and start listening to the answers that are "in here" – in your heart.

For you see, there is something else pre-encoded within you: the dreams and the wisdom of the heart. The wisdom of your soul whispers continuously to you, urging you to follow your deepest purpose.

You have universal signs that pop up right in front of you all the time – it's whether you 'choose' to see them or not. The interesting thing is that the Universe makes it so incredibly easy to rid yourselves of the old programming. Switch your focus and you'll start to become aware of the signs that spell out what "All That Is" is trying to tell you. You'll literally see the world differently.

Most people miss these signs because their minds are too busy looking at what their perceived reality is telling them – what they perceive as being in front of them at any given moment. But what is in front of us "right now" is only temporary – and always subject to change.

You can take control of that change.

In my case, when I was embroiled in my dysfunctional family situation, I was locked into this negative feedback seemingly coming from all around me in the outside world. However, these messages that I, along with most people, perceive as coming at us from outside are not the whole story.

There are many more messages available to us that, once we're awakened to them, give us a much clearer picture.

A much vaster, inner cache of messages is streaming out from our hearts, dreams and our "right connection" to the Universe at all times. That Universe wants us to achieve our true potential. It wants us be, do and have everything in our heart of hearts.

Before you start feeling inadequate about having been blind to your own potential and gifts, let me just say that there is nothing wrong with missing those messages. You might even say you are meant to miss them. It's all part of the challenge that is your experience here on Earth. You are designed to miss them because you have been given the potential to find a way to open your eyes. You're designed to go beyond whatever limitations you have perceived for yourselves.

The 'game' is difficult and challenging for a reason.

So even though your purpose is pre-encoded in your heart, everything is a creation of your thoughts. That means that when you start transforming thoughts to bring your minds in sync with the dreams in your heart, you become aligned with your purpose and are, therefore, in alignment with the Universe. When this happens, you are listening to the wisdom of your soul. Souls are the direct connection to the all-knowing and that is where all the answers exist.

THEY ARE ALSO LISTENING TO THEIR EGOS

The development of the ego is, in some respects, one of the greatest evolutionary human achievements. That's because, without the ego, we would not have fully developed self-reflective consciousness.

Animals, for example, do not have sharp, individualised egos like human beings. Bees and ants have hive mentality. They are not individuals, but rather, members of a group mind. Cows and sheep are herd animals. They don't have hive mentality like many insects but their group identity with the herd is dominant. They don't each have crystallised individual egos. As human beings, we do.

The huge price we pay for egos, however, is that they take over all aspects of our lives. The ego comes to think of itself as an all-powerful god, of sorts. If you mention the subconscious mind, the ego says:

"Subconscious mind? What subconscious mind? What a bunch of baloney!"

"Intuition? What a laugh! That's just a myth!"

"The dreaming minds? Well, dreams are fine, but they are not real! Most often they're just nonsense."

That's the way the ego 'thinks'. Every other aspect of our minds and consciousness is purely suspect. The ego self-anoints itself the be-all and end-all of everything we are – when in fact human beings are so much more.

The ego is also dominated by our intellect. It thinks that having a sky-high IQ is everything. Furthermore, the ego is extremely good at developing and nursing fear. Our egos fear everything. The reason for that is that the ego is hell-bent on survival – not just survival, but maintaining its dominant position of: "I'm the ego and I'm the only part of me that matters."

Another nasty habit of the ego is to form envy of others. The ego not only wants to dominate all aspects of your own consciousness, it also wants to outdo everyone else, be better than everyone else, have more fun, more money than everyone else. Plus, each ego wants to be perceived as the best damned ego on the planet.

This allows so much confusion to arise within us. It happens when people look at others and see what they are achieving in their lives. There always seems to be somebody who is smarter than you, better-looking than you, has a better love life than you, has more money than you, or who is enjoying life more than you – and so on and so on.

However, comparing yourself to other people is just another way of looking outside yourself for answers, whereas the only true answers that are specific to you are found within. When you envy another person, or compare yourself to another person, you are trying to live that person's dream and not your own dream.

Looking at others, trying to keep up with the Joneses, or trying to emulate a person you envy or admire, is destined to lead to failure. No other person's life, goals or dreams are better or worse than your own. There is no right or wrong – there's just "different". Other people are different from you. That's why you are unique!

There is a special place for everyone. No one else has lived the life you have lived or had the experiences you have had. You are a specialist on yourself! When it comes to "You", you're the expert. Also, no one is meant to miss out on their portion of happiness. There is always enough; there is something for everyone. Everyone has a dream, a dream that is unique to each individual.

Furthermore, it doesn't matter what you are doing, whether it be a role that is considered "humble" or something "significant" or "important". You might notice a lady selling flowers on a street corner. If she absolutely loves what she is doing, then that's what she is meant to do.

Our ego-dominated society would have us believe that selling flowers on the street is not as important as a heart surgeon saving lives, or an astronaut exploring outer space. But those are just arbitrary value judgements. Not everyone can be a heart surgeon or an astronaut. Not everyone can be the leader of their country, village or tribe.

Someone needs to wait tables and clean the bus station. Somebody needs to grow food on a farm and others need to haul trash to landfill. However, it's likely many people agree we do want someone to sell us beautiful flowers on the street to enrich our lives. Someone should do it! Every life, every job, every purpose matters.

Everyone is accomplishing their unique life plan at every moment and everything is always perfect. Life is a journey, not a destiny. Where you are at this moment and what you are doing now is always perfect – even if you don't like your situation. If you don't like where you are at this moment, then you have the power to change it.

WHAT IS YOUR TRUE PURPOSE?

Your true purpose is your lifelong dream. This goes beyond mere goals. Goals are the tools you use to reach certain short-term points in your life. Think of goals as pinpoints on a map, leading from one destination to another, and on and on. You use goals to get from Point A to Point B. Your true purpose, on the other hand, is the Big Picture. It is an ongoing journey.

When you are "on purpose", you will know it because you have that feeling of being fulfilled. You enjoy a natural feeling of clarity. Your heart sings as your soul guides your direction. You know your life has meaning and you experience life to the fullest. The Universe is working with you.

An integral aspect of true purpose is to love and to help, uplift and inspire those around you. Notice how this is opposite from ego-oriented thinking and behaviour. The Ego Self is always "all about me", and even further, the ego is "always striving to compete with and outdo" other people.

When you are resonating with your true purpose, you are thinking and acting in terms of cooperation. You think: "How can I get together with this other person to create a mutually beneficial scenario that will uplift both of us?" When you are in ego mode, you are thinking: "How can I dominate or screw over that other person so that I can get my winnings."

We are all connected to the One Universal Source which is pure energy and pure unlimited potential. We all share that energy. Everything is created from energy. That's why when you are fulfilling your true purpose your feeling of energy is endless.

When you are on purpose and following your true heart's dream, your energy seems to flow out of you naturally and effortlessly. You can jump out of bed at any moment and start doing what you love because you are inspired. Inspiration is a wellspring that flows from a direct connection with Universal Energy — which is always aligned with your true purpose.

When your energy is sluggish, it's a sign that you are not following the path of your heart's dream. It's not so much that the Universe is working against you; rather, think of it as the Universe telling you: "This is very difficult because you're not working on what you are supposed to be working on."

Everything is always in reflection – the Universe gives you what you 'want'. Your heart will sing as you work on your dream as it comes from inspiration (IN – SPIRIT – ION).

The Universe wants to work with you. It wants you to succeed. But it also wants you to accomplish this by using your own free will. It wants you to figure out a lot of things by yourself.

When you make the right choices, the Universe rewards you with abundant energy and feelings of joy. You feel that joy because you are in alignment with the Universe in terms of your purpose. When you go down an alternative path that seems 'wrong' at the time (although, there are truly no wrong paths) the Universe does not 'punish' you. Rather it actually gives you what you want. However, because you're out of alignment with your purpose, this 'success' will usually be a hollow victory that often leaves you feeling dissatisfied.

If you make true and positive choices, the Universe will gladly add to your energy and push you along. But remember: If you do seem to get bogged down it's only because you 'asked' for it. It is your way of having the exact experience you need on your journey to help push you towards your true purpose.

Those who follow their inner voice and vision make the greatest impact on the world. That also includes people who are involved in what many perceive as humble pursuits. It doesn't matter whether the difference you make is localised to a small community or affecting many people on a large scale. Yes, a woman selling flowers on a street corner can have a significant impact upon the world if she is doing what she loves to do. Having a positive influence and a "big impact" on the lives of others does not have to be groundbreaking or influencing broad strokes of history. If you're on the path of your true purpose, even the smallest contributions *matter* – it all makes a difference.

Chaos theory tells us that a tiny butterfly flapping its wings in the Amazon rainforest can set natural forces in motion that may eventually create a hurricane on the other side of the planet. Quantum mechanics tell us that the vibration of every atom and every molecule in the Universe sends a vibration that ripples throughout the entire Universe. There is no action so small or insignificant that it does not matter.

Thus, your true purpose in life is valid no matter how big or small your role is perceived to be by the rest of society. Life is not about accumulating money, achieving fame or

even generating endless feelings of happiness. It's about embracing and loving all sides of your physical experience, both the unhappy and the joyful. There will always be happiness and sadness, kindness and cruelty, success and failure to ever shifting degrees.

When you see both sides, accept both sides, you ignite a light in your soul that reflects the ultimate source of love – **love is the fundamental energy that powers the entire Universe.**

In fact, the fundamental purpose of Universal Consciousness is to constantly grow in love. Our spiritual journey is to awaken to that true love, as well as to do our part to generate love in our personal little corner of the Universe.

Just as each cell in the human body contributes to the overall health of the entire body, each human being, each individual contributes to the overall health of the entire Universe. When we strive to grow in love and find ways to make love stronger, better, more enriched and more refined, we add to the Universe's overall 'database' or storehouse of Love.

People often ask me: "What if I just don't know what my purpose is?"

The reality is that everyone knows their true purpose – even if it is hidden deep within you – because everyone has a dream. It's a gift we are born with. It's there! Believe me.

If people feel cut off from their dream there can be many reasons for it. However, it is most often because they are too focused on events that are happening outside themselves. They have come to believe that the events happening outside themselves are driving their fates, such as being 'trapped' within a dysfunctional family, or stuck in a dead-end job, or trapped in a loveless marriage.

People who feel cut off from their purpose are also ego-dominant. That doesn't necessarily mean you are acting out a powerful "ego maniac" type of existence. Being ego-dominant can mean you feel constantly victimised by fears and anxieties.

Have no doubt, an ego-dominant person can appear to be outwardly weak, stumbling and riddled with uncertainties. Ego-dominance can manifest in both the "control freak" personality and the "doormat personality". Both are basically acting out their fears with different coping mechanisms – the former with power and control, the other with constant submissiveness.

For example, if either of these personality types would adopt the practice of turning inward, of becoming quiet and listening to their own inner voices, they would discover that their souls are actually in a constant state of sending messages to their minds. The message from the soul is never: "Screw over that person before he screws you!" or, "Submit meekly to this situation or you'll be sorry!"

Rather, the message from the soul is more akin to:

"If you do this thing that you love and it helps others, you'll find a situation that is joyful, pleasant and meaningful."

We get little nudges all the time. This wisdom from our soul takes our perception of reality and links it to our purpose. When it integrates, our purpose becomes so alive it manifests the material aspects of our purpose into our physical reality.

Everyone is meant to experience an extraordinary life by finding a true essence within that is the power of God, the Universe, All That Is, the Larger Consciousness System, or whatever you want to call it. This power comes to you by way of an open heart which is the gateway to your soul – and the soul has all the universal information available to it, and thus to you.

That power is running through every single one of us. This in turn gives us the ability to manifest whatever desires the mind and heart hold as necessary and important.

If you understand that you actually possess the ability to live your dreams, what would they be? The more you strive to discover your dreams, and the more you take action to follow your inner dream to pursue what you love, more the Universe helps you and the more fulfilling your life becomes.

If the mind can perceive the dream in your heart, no matter how foolish it may seem, it is achievable. If it is in your awareness, then it can be manifested and accomplished.

Of course, there is a difference between wishful thinking and true purpose. There is also a difference between thinking about doing something and taking action. If you are just telling people about your true purpose but are doing nothing about it, then you are not taking solid steps in this physical world towards making your dream a reality. Unfortunately, you are drawing no universal energy into your creation. You won't be in alignment.

However, when you act upon your purpose – when you get out there and do it knowing you have no limitations — the

Universe will 'magically' provide the people, places and situations in order for you to fulfill your journey.

When you start to act on your dreams, when you take real solid action, you go from a state of just *believing* to a state of *knowing*. When you have that knowing, you are inspired and you gain an amazing sense of clarity.

When there is less doubt in your mind, less second-guessing, less dithering, you gain a sense of knowing that takes you beyond the limitations of your mind. You take control of your free will to make specific choices. When you have clarity of intent and take "right action", the Universe will respond every time and honour your states' desires by helping you achieve the goals you set forward, one after another.

I always say: You have to meet the Universe halfway. You can't sit around in the back garden or be a couch potato and say, "You know, this is what I would love", then do nothing about it. The Universe loves action. It says, "Yeah baby! Let me see you come out and do something!" When you get out there and go for it, you'll be amazed with the positive results.

Keep in mind that the Universe does not discriminate between what kinds of thoughts you hold most often.

If you constantly nurse limiting thoughts, the Universe will promptly oblige and limit you in the way you are thinking of being limited. This means you have to be really clear in your mind about what it is you want, where you want to go, what the dream in your heart is tugging you towards.

If you can find your dream, turn inwards, listen carefully to your heart, then become clear on your purpose in order to formulate the right intent, there is no stopping you! This is the formula to harnessing the unlimited energy of the Universe. The Universe is the ultimate reality-generating super machine. Set it straight and it will be at your beck and call, ready to deliver anything you program for yourself to achieve.

SUMMARY AND ACTION POINTS

Much of your life is pre-encoded by:

- Genetics.

- Pre-life planning/contracts.

- The "rule set" of your environment.

- The general archetype you belong to.

This means there are aspects of your life you cannot change. Example: Your height, eye colour, body shape, gifts and/or diseases you inherit from your gene pool.

You also have little or no control over the rule set of your environment. Example: You can't walk across the North Pole without a snowsuit because you'll freeze to death. You can't jump 100 feet high because the Law of Gravity is set in place. You can't walk through fire without getting burned.

While the above is set in stone, none of it is as powerful as the fact that:

YOU ALSO HAVE FREE WILL

- Free will allows you to change/control all of the important things, such as what you do, your level of joy, happiness and overall situation in life.

- If you are born into a dysfunctional family, you can escape that situation and change the way you react to it.

- You do not have to accept your "lot in life". You can shape it. If you hate your job, you can find another job which you love but still allows you to prosper.

- You control the way you think about everything that happens to you, for better or worse.

- You can start making choices with clarity of intent and purpose which will help you manifest exactly what you want in life.

YOU HAVE A DREAM IN YOUR HEART

If you are unclear about what your life means, what you are doing on this planet, or you don't understand why you are here, the answers are within you right now. The key is to learn to look within:

- Turn your mind inward in a contemplative, quiet and meditative way; you can learn to look into your heart where you will find all the answers you need.

- Your heart is whispering to you at all times, telling you what to do, and explaining your highest purpose.

- The more you learn to listen to your "Inner Voice" the more connected you will be to the "Universal Source" which wants to help you.

- The more you learn to trust your Inner Voice, the 'louder' that voice will become. The more you practise pursuing "right action", the higher your level of clarity.

- You will know when you are performing "right action" because you will feel naturally energised and experience greater levels of joy and satisfaction. The feedback that comes from within – joy, energy, peace and serenity – is more "real" and more important than what you perceive as "negative feedback" from "out there" outside yourself.

- The Universe wants you to succeed, it wants you to grow in love, it wants you to be kind, supportive and helpful to others. ***Cooperation* with others is superior to *competition* with others.**

CHAPTER 3

UNDERSTANDING AND DEFEATING FEAR

Now let's talk about a major issue: the Universal human phenomenon of fear.

In the previous chapter I talked about how we have many traits that are encoded within us genetically and for simply being human. One trait or aspect we are born with is the will to survive. It's instinctive. On a basic level, if we were not afraid of certain things, we'd soon be dead.

It's natural.

Consider a distant ancestor living in a cave. Before entering the mouth of that dark cave to explore it as a possible home, your early Stone Age ancestor would be crazy if he wasn't afraid of what might be lurking in the darkness. Maybe a gigantic bear is in there that would love to eat him for lunch so he'd be darned careful before entering for the first time.

His fear of a natural enemy is a basic survival mechanism. It makes sense to be afraid of a sabre-tooth tiger, a man-eating shark or a lion. We have the scary equivalent of sabre-toothed cats lurking in our modern world today. You might fear muggers lying in wait around corners, on dark streets or in questionable areas of your neighbourhood. The media often reports terrorists bombing innocent people around the globe in the name of religion, leadership struggles or war.

There appears to be an endless amount of objects, people and events to be fearful about. The nightly news often plays out like a horror story – with all the macabre trimmings. Perhaps climate change will ruin our planet. What about nuclear war? Maybe the pesticides in the food we eat will give us cancer. It's only a matter of time before an earthquake swallows your city. The murder/crime rate is on the rise in your town!

Think of all the major and minor fears that permeate our lives. It doesn't always have to be a life-threatening fear. A lot of people are afraid they'll lose their jobs or lose their homes if they can't pay their mortgages. Other people are afraid of being abandoned by a spouse or lover. Still others fear something as simple as being alone, or missing out. Some people are terrified of public speaking – and let's not forget phobias.

OUR SOCIETY SELLS FEAR

If the nightly news is not frightening enough, there is another more insidious and even more pervasive source of fear in our lives – advertising.

Just turn on the TV, watch the commercials and find out how inadequate you are, how behind the times you are, how out of fashion you are and how much you have to fear in your world.

It goes on and on. Fearful programming and advertising messages are not only on television; they can be found everywhere in our environment, saturating our lives. Highway billboards, the radio in your car, newspaper and magazine ads, endless Internet ads popping up on your screen, spam emails, junk mail in your mailbox... the merchants of fear are everywhere! Even if you tried living under a rock, you'd probably still see a skywritten advertising message trying to lure potential customers to buy an item 'the Joneses' already own.

The big advertising firms learned long ago that fear sells.

They also know that in order to get you to buy, they need to make you feel inadequate. They need to convince you that you have a significant problem right now, whether you know it or not. If you don't have a problem, don't worry – they'll create one for you. Then they'll turn around and sell you something to fix the problem you didn't know you had.

IT'S TIME TO TAKE BACK YOUR SERENITY AND SANITY

The first step in defeating fear is to recognise it and have greater awareness of where it's all coming from. We all grew up in a media-saturated environment. Media experts tell us that advertising is our "primary form of public address". We know for a fact that advertising is a heavy purveyor of fear.

Most of us just take the messages we are bombarded with for granted. "It's just life," we think. We don't even think about it that much. Sure, we all know that advertisers fabricate, stretch the truth, exaggerate and outright lie. They will do anything they can get away with to persuade us, night and day, to buy something. That's why we take everything with a grain of salt – or at least we tell ourselves we do.

The American philosopher and psychologist William James said:

"There's nothing so absurd that if you repeat it often enough, people will believe it."

Or as the Russian revolutionary Vladimir Lenin said:

"A lie told often enough eventually becomes the truth."

The lesson in these statements is that repetition seeps into the human mind whether you want it to or not. Sure, you may be largely ignoring all the advertising, but it just keeps hammering away.

Experts also say:

> *"The subconscious mind does not know the difference between the truth and a lie."*

So even if you are ignoring or discounting the negative, fearful media messages saturating our lives, some of them are still getting through. Your subconscious mind is absorbing the constantly repeated messages of doom, problems and inadequacy. So for reasons that aren't really that odd when you think about it, we begin to feel fearful and uncertain in our lives.

Then there's the nightly news. That's not advertising – that's journalists telling us like it is, right? Just the facts. Right? It's even more difficult to discount or downplay the fearful news stories we must confront every day because we consider this to be factual information. How do you ignore the hard reality of crime in your neighbourhood or greedy corporations dumping toxic chemicals in the water or the latest story of war or famine in some inflamed corner of the world?

Once again, the media is just giving its own version of what's happening in the world and much of this is fabricated to meet a desired result – not necessarily the events, but the 'spin'.

Again, it all begins with awareness. Here is the solid truth:

Most of the fears we harbour within ourselves are pure delusion.

They're not real.

No matter how real or pervasive your fears may seem, you need to come to grips with the amazing reality that there really isn't all that much to fear in our daily lives. Often, there is absolutely nothing to be afraid of.

Fear is an assumption in the imagination that in the future one will experience more losses than gains, more pains than pleasures, more negatives than positives. It's the assumption that something bad is bound to happen to you, thoughts such as "I might get mugged" or "fired from my job" or "catch a bad disease". It hasn't happened yet – but it might!

Fear is always about the future. You fear things that haven't happened yet – and are unlikely to happen to you personally. It's as though you pay the same price if something bad happens or not – because you spend too much of your Now (your Present Moment) worrying about fears that might come at you in the future.

This is true whether there is a very high or very low probability of some terrible event happening to you.

However, if we do everything we can to foster, nurture and grow fearful events then the risk of them actually occurring increases. Fear – like any other thought, feeling or value we hold in our minds – is a magnet for itself.

When you consider the reality of the Law of Reflection, everything that is in your life right now is something you have created and magnetised to yourself. If you have been nursing a lot of fears, fears of all kinds, shapes and sizes, you probably find that a lot of the things you fear enter your life.

The more you look at fears, listen to fears, examine fears and dwell on fears – the more you magnetise these fears into your personal sphere of operation. Then, after you did everything you could (by constantly thinking about fear) to make sure something fearful happens, you say:

> *"See, I told you I wasn't just being paranoid. It really did happen. I was right to be afraid!"*

It's a self-fulfilling prophecy. You get trapped in a never-ending vicious cycle of fear, magnetising those fears to yourself, then checking the feedback and validating your belief system. You live in a fearful world and you constantly work to prove it to yourself. Most of the time, you do it without knowing you are doing it.

HOW DO WE STOP "FEARING"

You don't have to live your life in fear. You can change.

You can stop being fearful, stop listening to outside sources that are telling you to be fearful and adopt an attitude of basic common sense. Such as: right now, where you are sitting and reading this, you have very little to be fearful about. That is your Present Moment, your Now, and it's this Present Moment that matters.

STOP TUNING INTO FEAR – TUNE OUT

A lot of people who are working on their own spiritual growth and advancement today tell me they have simply stopped reading newspapers and watching the nightly news. They have done so because they have decided the only way to win the game is to "not play" the game. That is, there seems to be little or nothing we can do about all the wars and violence happening around the world, all the ignorance and confusion, all the poverty and societal degradation. Thus, they choose to just "let it go", and ignore it.

Some might say this is the "ostrich approach" — sticking one's head in the sand and pretending nothing bad is happening. Hoping it will "all go away" is dangerous, so the sceptics say, because if you simply stop listening to all the bad news you'll be uninformed. Ignorance is not a solution, the sceptics add. By simply ignoring all the bad news, you leave yourself less prepared to cope with bad events if and when they happen to you.

Note, I said "sceptics": constantly tuning into and constantly dwelling on the frightening daily news is not a solution either.

In fact, it is worse.

That's because by constantly feeding into the "fear cycle" of the daily news and becoming attached to those scary stories, you are literally plunging yourself into the endlessly revolving loop of absorbing bad news, feeling bad and afraid about it, then magnetising all that bad stuff into your own life. In fact, you may end up contributing to it, willingly or unwillingly.

When one person starts to live his or her life in fear, it's contagious. Other people around you will pick up on your fear – then they start acting fearfully towards you and others. As more fear spreads, the further it reaches throughout your neighbourhoods and the rest of society.

Whether you decide to tune into the news of the world or not, the important thing is you don't allow the fearful news to 'stick' to you. It's important to remind yourself that you, as an individual (as an "Individuated Unit of Consciousness" in the Universe), have a far greater ability to control what happens in your personal world than you imagined.

As difficult as it is to believe, you, personally, do not have to be affected by all the bad news that seems to be swirling around "out there" in the rest of the world.

The famous psychic Jane Roberts, who spent years channelling the hyper-intellectual entity Seth, makes a good point about fearful events that are occurring around the world. Seth said that when we read about wars or other fearful events in other parts of the world, such as natural disasters or famines, it's a good idea to try to separate everything into two categories:

1. The events that are in your Primary Reality.

2. The events that are in your Secondary Reality.

Generally, the really bad things we see on TV or read about are occurring somewhere else, not at your doorstep, or even in your city or neighbourhood. Those terrible events are happening in your Secondary Reality. A Secondary Reality is a level removed from your Primary or Personal Reality, which means you already have a reason to put these fears on the backburner, so to speak.

In order to stay tuned into your own Primary Reality, start by unloading the fears out of your life. It's unlikely you can do much to change the outcomes in your perceived Secondary Reality, which is probably happening in some distant corner of the planet, so try to let it go for now.

Okay, so what about fearful events that might be happening in your Primary Reality? Well, the good news about this is you have a great deal of control over what happens to you, what you confront and what your outcomes will be in your own Primary Reality. You have way more personal control over your Primary Reality than your Secondary Reality.

Your personal Primary Reality follows the shape and form of your thoughts and intentions. If you keep positive, loving, kind, peaceful and prosperous thoughts front and centre in your Primary Reality, believe me, you will be consistently confronted by a positive, loving, kind, peaceful and positive world – in your Primary Reality.

Let me repeat:

You create your own reality.

You magnetise people, objects and situations into your life based on your own thoughts.

The fewer thoughts of fear, hopelessness and despair you hold front and centre in your mind, the less fear, hopelessness and despair you will experience in life.

By keeping positive, life-giving and joyful thoughts at the forefront of your mind, you will receive more positivity, life-enriching and happy experiences in your life.

THE ULTIMATE FEAR REMEDY

One of the most powerful ways to reduce your own mental, internal fear cycle is to try to quiet the mind and stop the incessant, internal chatter constantly running through your head.

The best way to foster a more serene mind and to rid yourself of incessant negative thoughts, negative thinking and internal chatter is to practise some form of daily meditation.

I do not mean you need to take up a formal discipline, such as TM (Transcendental Meditation), or Zen Meditation, or Tantric Yoga Meditation – or run off to India to find a guru and join his ashram for the next 10 years.

The best meditation is actually quite simple and extremely uncomplicated. Anyone can do it! It's free and available to every person on the planet. All it involves is finding quiet time for 10 to 20 minutes per day, when you can sit in an uninterrupted place so you can practise calming your mind and letting go of your thoughts.

Usually this means sitting or lying down and focusing all of your awareness on your breathing. Make each breath deep, slow and natural. Most people who try this for the first time are amazed to discover that the Mind is actually deeply affected by the way we breathe. Our mind takes cues from how rapidly and shallow we breathe (fear, stress, anxiety) and how leisurely and deeply we breathe (calm, serene, peaceful).

The tenor of the Mind follows the lead of the breath.

Now, many people quickly discover that when they sit down to meditate and focus on their breathing, their thoughts seem to have a mind of their own. Thoughts keep clamouring their chatter, coming at you and refuse to shut off. It seems that this "meditation thing" is not working at all.

The key is not to struggle against your thoughts. Don't force them to go away or try to force them by shaping your thoughts in one direction or another. It just doesn't work that way. Troublesome thoughts are like flypaper or a sticky spider's web. The more you struggle against them, the more entangled you become.

Rather, just let your thoughts come and go without becoming attached to them. Simply observe your thoughts. Watch them like passing clouds in the sky. Don't get attached to any single line of thought, or any particular thought. Just keep allowing each thought to come, then go. Let them march along like a parade, while you stand by watching the spectacle. Relax and let it flow.

What you'll soon (eventually) notice is that this process has a calming effect. As your thoughts march by – and you gently keep your primary focus on your breathing – you'll find your mind will become quieter and more serene, more peaceful and less involved in struggle.

The further effect of this is fewer and fewer fearful thoughts. Yes, you may still have fearful thoughts even while meditating, but now you are learning not to be so attached to them. When you become less attached to fearful thoughts, guess what? They start to lose their power over you.

Not only that but they will eventually go away altogether – or at least for longer periods of time during your days. That's definitely an improvement on being fearful all day.

Less time spent harbouring and nursing negative and fearful thoughts means you are literally transforming your world – transforming your very existence – into a more positive, joyful and loving kind of world. You'll enjoy a world in which good things seem to be happening to you, more and more.

It's my intention here to only touch on the subject of meditation. Indeed, whole books have been written on the topic. In fact, the number of books available on meditation alone could probably fill an entire library.

What I want you to know is that meditation is one of the most powerful tools to help you conquer fear. The best part is it's available to anyone. Use meditation daily to rid yourself of fear and help turn your mind towards more positive, loving, peaceful and serene thoughts.

If you want to take formal training with one of the many schools of meditation, be it TM or Zen, Yogic or a purely secular method – by all means, I encourage that. Any one of the above methods can be used as a powerful tool to stop the fear cycle. You can also achieve great results from just taking it upon yourself to sit quietly a couple of times a day to focus on your breathing and calm your mind.

ACCEPTANCE

Another way to conquer fear is acceptance – acceptance of the fact that, yes, the worst might happen to you. At first this might sound counter-intuitive but let me give you some examples to illustrate what I mean by this.

Let's say that, for some reason, you will be required to give a public speech. Maybe it is a presentation to your co-workers or you have been asked to speak at a social event for a group you belong to such as a business club or charity organisation.

We all know that public speaking can be one of some people's biggest fears. In fact, many people report that only physical death is more frightening than the idea of having to give a speech.

So right away, you have a huge amount of fear developing:

What if I make a fool of myself?

What if people don't like what I have to say?

What if I come off looking like an idiot?

What if people are so bored they start walking out during my speech?

What if people start criticising the way I'm dressed?

What if they don't like me?

Okay, these are genuine fears. But since you are required to give the speech anyway (let's say you can't get out of it no matter what) the first thing you should do is accept that the worst might happen.

If the worst does happen, then it happens, then there is little you can do to change it anyway. You created it by thinking it.

Rather, if you take another attitude that says:

> *"Okay, maybe I'll make a major idiot out of myself or maybe I won't. In either case, I just have to go through with it."*

Once you take this accepting attitude, you have already taken the first step towards overcoming the power that fear holds over you. You have addressed it head-on. You have not run for cover or cowered behind a bush – feeding even more power to your fear.

Once you adopt an attitude of acceptance, you have stopped fighting and struggling. When you stop fighting and struggling, your natural energy can flow more easily. You will find it easier to allow the flow of the Universe – which is always supporting you and only wants the best for you – into your world.

You accept what is, but you don't resign to it. Instead, you decide to look fear squarely in the eye, confront it, address it, then just go out there and do your best. You gain a victory over fear before it can gain control over you.

Always ask yourself in any fearful situation:

"What's the worst that can happen to me?"

Let's say you are fearful of walking into your boss' office and asking for a pay raise so you keep putting it off, week after week, month after month.

Now ask yourself:

"If I walk into my boss' office and ask for a pay raise or promotion, what's the worst that can happen to me?"

Of course, about the worst thing that can happen to you is you will be told "No". You might be disappointed, but the experience is not going to kill you – and at least you tried. You'll feel better about yourself for trying rather than if you sat back and let the opportunity go by.

It doesn't matter what the situation is. In order to defeat fear, you must prepare to accept the worst. What you'll discover is, the worst almost never happens. In fact, the more you accept the consequences of fear, the less powerful fear becomes – and you'll likely encounter fewer terrible outcomes.

Acceptance allows you to break the cycle of fear. Instead of being caught in a vicious loop of fearing, magnetising fear then acknowledging that fearful things happen, you go forward with courage. You will expect the best and receive the best outcomes then enjoy the feedback that comes from all the great things that are happening in your life.

The Law of Reflection will show itself in true form. Your life will reflect more and more happy and positive outcomes.

FEAR IS THE OPPOSITE OF LOVE

The opposite of love is not hate. The opposite of love is fear.

Hate is a byproduct of fear. We hate other people, other groups, other races, other political parties, other nations because we fear them. We put up defences against those people, groups and situations we fear. They react in kind and the situation goes from bad to worse. Taking a defensive posture based on fear makes it extremely difficult to love others.

Thus, one of the primary ways to defeat fear is to strive to become a more loving person every day – *in every way in your life*. Hold loving thoughts in your mind and make your actions reflect this loving way of thinking.

When you show forth love and do loving works, you reduce fear in others. The result is they start to direct more positive, loving outcomes in your direction.

This is the wisdom behind "Love thy enemy".

Again, sceptics, who like to call themselves "realists", rave against this notion. They say it is naïve to love your enemy because that only allows them to take advantage of you. To show love is to display "weakness", they say. These are the kinds of people who think Charles Darwin's law of "survival of the fittest" is what really drives everything on our planet.

Fearful people love to quote Darwin – out of context, of course. What they fail to understand is that Charles Darwin himself considered "survival of the fittest" to be only a minor part, or subset, of the way he viewed the natural process of evolution.

Darwin's first book, *On the Origin of the Species,* spent a lot of time explaining the survival of the fittest. It was published in 1859. However, in his second book, *The Descent of Man*, published in 1871, Darwin spent a lot of time talking about how "love and cooperation" were far more important to the advancement of a species than "strife and competition".

Even today, it's amazing how so many so-called 'experts' love to talk about Darwin's first book, but completely ignore his more advanced and complete theory of evolution published 12 years later in his second book.

Darwin noted that those species that cooperated and helped each other the most tended to have the strongest chance at survival. Not only that, but they were able to thrive.

It's not only good science, it's common sense. People who help each other and support each other have far more opportunities to achieve better outcomes in their lives. Two heads are better than one! When people get together in groups, neighbourhoods, charities, non-profit groups and all the rest, they can do amazing things.

Just the opposite is true when people fight and compete with each other. In that scenario, you always have a winner and a loser – but a lot of the time, you really have two losers. Nobody wins from war.

Again, this goes back to fear being the opposite of love. Love is a binding force. It brings people and situations together so they cooperate for the greater good of all.

Stop dwelling on fear! Cultivate loving thoughts, feelings and attitudes. Direct this love inward toward yourself and outward toward others. Love is the most fundamentally powerful force in the Universe. In your daily life, you cannot afford to ignore this most basic source of positive energy. You need to give and accept as much love as you can every day.

The Law of Reflection will easily show you that love is a highly reflective material.

The more you give out, the more it reflects back to you – and it can make amazing, positive changes in all areas of your life, both big and small.

You may even want to contemplate the quality of love on a more profound and direct way in your moments of quiet meditation.

The great spiritual teacher Ram Das once suggested a mantra that people could repeat to themselves over and over again: "How do I love?" By dwelling on this question, you can send yourself into a deeper understanding of just what love is, how it feels and how you can 'grow' more of it into your life.

For example, all of us certainly have someone or something in our lives right now that we love. Therefore we clearly recognise that "love feeling" or love quality. Think about the love you have for your spouse, your partner, your children or a close friend. Although, it could be something else – such as the love you have for your pet – or even your love for the taste of chocolate.

A terrific exercise is to choose a source of love in your life – something you clearly love, and do so without a doubt – then dwell on the quality and feeling of that love.

For example, let's just say you love your cat. In a quiet moment of meditation, attempt to bring your attention to that feeling of love you have for your cat. Whatever you do, do not intellectualise it!

That is, don't think to yourself: "I love my cat because she sleeps at the foot of my bed and purrs at night." That's an intellectual reason or "item" that makes you love your cat.

Rather, try to get out of your mind and feel the sense of love you have for your cat at your core level.

Focus your attention on your centre – your stomach area, solar plexus and chest – and notice how the love for your cat creates a sensation in this area, a sensation that is pure awareness. It's not even necessarily an emotional feeling I am talking about but the most basic, fundamental perception of what "love for my cat" feels like from a standpoint of pure awareness.

Choose any target or object of love you like. For example, it may be easier for you to focus on your love for a child or spouse, a grandparent or favourite aunt. The idea is to search your awareness of exactly what that love feels like, or how it seems to be manifesting in your consciousness.

This simple exercise will help you become more deeply connected to what love itself actually is, and how it seems to be entering your being – not just your mind and emotions – but your central sense of awareness at the most fundamental level.

The deeper understanding you gain from dwelling on love in such a contemplative way will make you stronger in the power of love. It will grow more freely and liberally in your mind, heart, emotions and awareness. The more you foster the very essence and quality of love in your awareness, the more it will blossom outward into all aspects of your life.

Since love is the opposite of fear, the more deeply you go into love, and cultivate it in your awareness at the being level, the more it will push out fear – and very soon, you'll find absolutely amazing things happening in your life.

SUMMARY AND ACTION POINTS

The Law of Reflection makes it obvious that if you dwell on fears, pay attention to fear and nurture fear in your life, then that is what will be reflected back to you. You will have a lot of fearful events in your life.

It's important to break the cycle of fear. You do that by:

- Tuning out all of the fear and negativity that is coming at you from the media, including news and advertising.

- Choosing to simply ignore all the bad news; better yet, don't let it 'stick' to you. You can stay informed, but you don't have to buy into all that fear.

- Remembering that awareness is the key. Try to be aware of the outside media sources, especially advertisers and marketers that are constantly attempting to scare you into buying something. When you become aware of this intent among others, you can discount it, and not let it sink in, consciously or subconsciously.

MAJOR FEAR REMEDIES ARE:

- Meditation – Learn to calm your mind and rid yourself of internal 'chatter'. Much of that chatter is fear-based and repetitive. Once you reduce it, you will grow far less fearful.

- Acceptance – When you are willing to accept the idea that the worse can happen in any situation, yet remain willing to move forward anyway, you take the power away from fear. Accept the possibility that the worst might happen but have the courage to push forward. Remember, you always create the outcome.

- Love – The very opposite of fear is love. The more you foster feelings of love within yourself and project it towards others, the more fear will be reduced in your life and the world you perceive.

CHAPTER 4

> *"Only you have the power to change your reality"*
>
> **A**LIDA FEHILY

FINDING YOUR TOP VALUES

If you want to change your life for the better, the Law of Reflection can help you find the perfect starting point from which to get this done.

When you start well you end up in a better place.

It's better than just flailing around at random – trying this and that, using trial and error, hoping you get out of the situation you are in right now and onto something better – without putting in the work.

Think of it like an archer practising with a bow and arrow. If she does not know where she is standing in relation to her target, how can she take good aim? An archer not only needs to have a clear eye on her mark, she must have a sense of her total environment.

For example, on any given day a certain amount of wind is blowing across the archery range. A crosswind can nudge or sway the flight path of an arrow. Knowing which way the wind is blowing can help the archer compensate by aiming slightly left or right to counter the effect of the wind.

An archer must also work on her stance. She must have her feet planted firmly on the ground so she is in a solid position to shoot from a firm foundation. Of course, an archer has an eye on her goal. She knows exactly where she wants the arrow to strike.

If you don't have a solid idea of exactly where your goal is, it's like shooting while wearing a blindfold or trying to see through dense fog.

Thus, to get to a better place in your life, you must take the time to determine the totality of where you are right now. You need to know where you stand and gather as much knowledge about what is influencing your situation. You need to develop a clear vision of where you want to go and a better idea of where you want to end up.

YOU CREATED IT ALL

As I have already mentioned, when you take an honest and unflinching look at where you are right now, your challenge is to come to grips with the fact that everything in your life is of your own creation. You manifested it all. That's the Law of Reflection. Your total environment – where you stand right now, what surrounds you – is that which you have drawn to yourself.

You have orchestrated all of it, as if you were a novelist writing a book, using yourself as the main character.

However, a real novelist writing mere fiction has the advantage. They know absolutely everything about their fictional character, as well as the total environment that character is operating within. That's because the writer has painstakingly created every aspect of that character's world, word-by-word and sentence-by-sentence.

A good novelist usually starts with an outline – they map out everything that is going to happen in their book before they start Chapter One. They may also create a complete profile for each character – even write a resume for each character – before they insert them into the narrative and plot.

In contrast, people in reality often behave like amateur novelists who are just winging it, making up stuff as they go along. They have a vague idea of their own life story but very little is planned or examined.

If a fiction writer did that, he or she would soon run into trouble. Most of the time the result of a poorly planned book is that the author writes his or herself into a corner. The result is that the plot breaks down. The writer gets stuck and the novel is never completed. Or the writer just keeps winging it and keeps adding pages that tend to wander without plot. The author might throw in action scenes that don't make sense. The result will be a body of writing that never really gels into a coherent story. Soon, the reader loses interest.

Again, most people live like that. They get up every day with only a vague idea of what they are going to do, why they are doing what they do and what they ultimately want to accomplish.

Fortunately, (or unfortunately) most people are riding along in pre-determined moulds that have been created for them by others – by society.

For example, you know you have to go to your job. You have to arrive by 9am. You have to do X amount of work, complete Task A and Task B, take lunch at noon, clock out at 5pm. Arriving home, you continue to do all of the non-work things that society expects of you such as making dinner for your family, cleaning the house, attending the school board meeting, engaging in hobbies or whatever you do in your non-work time.

Often, most people have no idea how they got into the routine they are in. At the same time, millions of people feel that they are hopelessly "caught in a rut". They are doing all the things that society expects them to do but it feels dreary, boring and alienating. People wonder if there's something better, more interesting and more fulfilling to do with their lives.

How many people have asked themselves in bewilderment: "How did I get trapped in this marriage?"

Or they say, "I'm stuck in this job but I need the money, and I don't know how to get out."

Or, "How did my life come to this?"

Or, "I never planned to be _____."

The answer is: You create everything that is in your life right now. (I know I sound like a broken record, but I need to drum this point home and keep repeating it to ensure you get the right message.)

People become stuck in ruts because they created a life for themselves without paying much attention to what they were doing. They are vaguely allowing themselves to be carried along by the natural flow of the societal mould, along with the belief system they were born into. Often, people get up every day and do what was required of them (most of the time) but for the most part they have not been actors but reactors.

Maybe you have been living your life like a novelist writing a story without an outline, with only a vague idea of your own plot. You're like an archer flinging arrows through a fog. Sometimes you hit your goal through blind luck but most of the arrows in your quiver are wasted or squandered.

So the key to changing your life is to stop, take stock of where you are right now and figure out what your top values are.

THE EXAMINED LIFE

It was the ancient Greek philosopher Plato who said:

"The unexamined life is not worth living."

Actually, Plato was quoting his great teacher, Socrates.

In keeping with this theme, this is what was inscribed upon the Temple of Apollo at Delphi:

"Know Thyself."

It was at Delphi that the famous Oracle Cave was located, where people would go, sometimes travelling hundreds of kilometres, to find inner wisdom and to figure out what they should do with their lives.

Your challenge is to come to "Know Thyself" if you are ever going to get out of your rut and start creating the life of your dreams. You don't have to travel to a cave in Greece to get the job done. You can start right now just by sitting down with a pen and a clean sheet of paper, or a blank computer screen. It's a terrific idea to start writing down details about your life – making everything vivid right there in front of you.

Getting in touch with who you are, where you are and where you want to go is vital to achieving a more joyful, meaningful existence. An existence that makes sense to yourself, one that brings you into sync with the Universe. An existence that helps you do exactly what you came to this Earthly existence to do.

TAKE A GOOD LOOK AT YOURSELF

Start by taking a look at yourself – the "Reflection" of what you have already created – so you can take stock of where you are standing right now. Again, you might want to start writing all this down now, or at least plan to do so later.

For example:

What do you spend the bulk of your time on?

What takes up the majority of your time every day?

I know a man who says his children are the most important thing in his life but when I asked him to tell me what he spent the majority of his time on, he said: "That's easy – work."

Then I asked: "Okay, what do you generally do when you get home from work?"

He said: "To be honest, I have to admit I watch TV every night as a general rule – I'm too tired out from working all day to do much else."

I asked: "What else do you do after work?"

He said: "Sometimes I work out in the yard or do chores around the house. I have some activities I do with friends – I'm in a bowling league, for example."

Then I asked: "How much time would you say you spend with your children?"

He said: "Well, the kids are just around all the time so I just interact with them naturally. I talk to them when I get home. We try to have family dinners together as often as we can. I help them with their homework sometimes, that kind of thing. But they're often off doing their own things."

So here we see a man who believes his children are his Number One priority in life. However, when it gets down to brass knuckles, he spends the vast majority of his time doing something other than interacting with his kids. His priorities are work, watching television and a few other miscellaneous activities.

I'm not saying there is anything wrong with this. His situation is probably entirely typical and even a somewhat happy situation. The point is, when people really take the time to examine their values, such as the value of time, they will find out that their own, personal top priority is not what they think it is. This man's top priority is his work, based on how he uses his time. That's just a fact.

Some might argue: He works all the time because his kids are his top priority and working long hours is his way of manifesting that because he is providing financial stability. That might be true but it's neither here nor there in terms of what we are talking about. The hard fact is his work is taking up most of his time – thus, his life is going to manifest accordingly.

Let's take another example of self-examination. Let's look at some of the things in your environment. For example, if you are a reader, what kind of books do you read? If you go take a look at all of the titles on your personal bookshelf – or the titles listed in your e-book reader – what are the majority of them about?

What kind of music do you listen to?

What do you talk about most with your friends, family, spouse and co-workers? How often do you pay attention to your own conversations? What subjects do you find yourself returning to again and again?

What subject dominates your inner dialogue? What do you think about most? Several times a day, stop to take note of what you are dwelling upon. Here is where keeping a notebook or journal can provide stunning revelations. So many people who have tried this have been amazed to find out what is really on their own minds, without realising it.

This exercise can be a sobering experience. It can also be an incredibly enlightening experience.

What do you spend most of your money on? Are you a saver or a spender? Do you spend money on books, clothing, stocks or bonds, travel or entertainment? Maybe all your money goes into paying your mortgage or your car payments? What do you spend your extra cash on? Do you buy things you don't need but you purchase them just because you want to? Where you are choosing to channel the bulk of your "money energy" says a lot about how you are manifesting your own reality.

In what areas of life are you the most organised? This will be one of your most important values. That's because you tend to find that which is most important to you in those areas in which your life is most organised. Good organisation is a sign you have put a lot of tender loving care into the details of that activity or aspect of your life. It takes attention and care to organise and stay organised. It means you have to constantly add energy to keep things in order. If you are choosing to expend a lot of energy on something, it means you place a high value upon it.

What are your goals? There are both short-term goals and long-term goals. An amazing amount of people draw a blank on this question. More often, they list some very vague goals that are long-term, but they have no real plan to help them achieve those goals.

Personally, I think many self-help gurus place too much emphasis on goals. That's because I see life as a journey and all of us are always on our journey. We're going somewhere whether we know it or not. It's the long haul – the whole shebang! Goals are important, yes, but they are short-term tools that help us get from Point A to Point B. At the same time, goal-setting behaviour is a proven, powerful tool.

Right now, we are trying to figure out what are our values and where we have been placing our energy so we can figure out how our lives have come to reflect the reality we find ourselves immersed within.

What are the 10 most important things in your life? Do you think you could list them? It may be easy for some and tough for others. Examples of the 10 most important things in life for most people are items such as money, health, love, relationships, work, artistic pursuits or visions, finding peace, religion and/or spirituality, fun/hobbies/free time – things like that.

Another good exercise is to make a list of the 10 things you really love to do. It may not be something you are doing right now but something you have always wished you could do or want to do.

BE, DO, HAVE

Creating a "Be, Do, Have" list is yet another helpful way to be clear on what you want in life. I already asked you to list the things you love. Now, write down the elements you would love to have in your life. It might be a wide variety of items such as money, clothing, jewellery, travel, the perfect partner, a new house that's paid for, and so on.

Then you have to ask yourself: In order for me to have these things in my life, what do I have to do?

For example, in my case, I'm a writer, a speaker, a wisdom consultant, Esoteric Chaperone™, an intuitive consultant, and so forth. So that's what I "Do". To do what I do, I first have to be that which can do. That is, in order to work as a wisdom consultant, I must have developed that skill to such a level that someone else will pay me money to receive the benefit of my consultations. In order to make money selling a book, I first have to be a writer, undertake the writing then I can earn income from the sale of my books.

Then comes the "Have" part. Through being what I am, and doing what I do, I can have what I want for myself in this life.

However, the important aspect of this formula is the order: Be, Do, Have. Most people dwell on what they want to HAVE without stopping to think about what they have to DO to get those things, and what they have to BE in order to be able to DO.

Ancient wisdom tells us that it is important to start with the BE.

For example, if your job is working as a burger flipper at a fast food restaurant for minimum wage, this is what you have selected as your BE – you are BEING a minimum wage burger flipper. As a low-paid fast food worker, it is unlikely that your HAVE list is going to come into your life through what you are DOING by BEING what you are BEING. On the other hand, that person's HAVE list may not include luxury items; thus, the HAVE list they have will come into BEING.

Keep in mind, working at a minimum wage job may be just right for you and allow you to have just what you need in life to be joyful, peaceful and happy. People who work for minimum wages may not have much in terms of material possessions but they may have far less in the way of responsibilities, stresses and risks in their working lives. If such people live simply, they can also live in an extremely happy state.

Next, look into your past. Go back year-by-year, all the way to your earliest childhood memories. What is the first thing you remember? What are the most significant memories from your childhood? What really stands out? What kind of events happened to you that really shaped your future, in your opinion?

Going through your entire life is obviously a monumental task. I'm not saying you should record every minute of what you can recall from your first hazy memories of being a toddler through your childhood, teenage years, and so on. But it is helpful in this task of gaining a better perspective on "Knowing Thyself".

A rigorous re-examination of your entire life and childhood can help give you a perspective on who you are, why you are here, and how you got to be where you are today, as well as the person you are now.

TAKE A LOOK AT YOUR OWN LIFE STORY

Taking a closer look at where you came from, where you have been and what you are preoccupied with today is all part of a process that will help you begin to start planning where you intend to go from here.

If you want, you can change everything. Many of you may like a lot of what you see about yourself. You'll have pleasant memories of childhood and other events throughout your life. Others will find much that is painful and perhaps even soaked in regrets. Many people, such as myself, suffered abusive childhoods that perhaps we would rather forget. Many such people will feel they have been victimised by life, especially if they were abused as children. They feel bitter and cheated.

They say:

> *"I didn't ask to be abused as a child. I was young, helpless and innocent. I will always be damaged for life as a result!"*

It doesn't have to be that way. That's because where you are right now – the Present Moment – "The Now" – is the ultimate locus of power of your entire existence.

Think of it as if you are standing on the peak of a mountain. You look down the descending slope on one side and that is the past. You turn to the other side and see another descending slope – that is the future. The "Present Moment" is the peak – where you are right now. It is from this location you can gain control of both what is behind you and what is before you.

The past does not matter as much as the Present Moment. The future is not as powerful as the Present Moment. You are in the Present Moment right now which means you can be the architect of your entire existence.

As I said, I was abused as a child, but I don't let that control who and what I am today. I have a choice. Rather than wallow in the past and decry the terrible things that happened in my earliest, most vulnerable years, I know I am in charge of creating my entire reality today. I now see my childhood as a blessing and would not change it. That's because it has shaped me into who I am today.

There is also this: All of us enter this world with a pre-planned destiny. If terrible things happen to us, seemingly due to outside sources that are attacking us for no reason, well, that's not the entire story. We all seek the challenges we want in this lifetime as part of our soul planning. Even before we are born we have helped to plan situations for ourselves, sometimes of great and indescribable pain, which are designed to help us learn and grow.

We can't lose sight of the fact that all of us are immortal. The soul always survives, no matter how harsh or terrible the tribulation. We may have breezed through this life with happy magical childhoods and a lifetime of prosperity, love and good health. Or perhaps, we started out in poverty, abuse and dreariness then proceeded through a painful life. Either way, we have survived it all and gone on to keep learning, experiencing and playing in the Universe.

The point I want to end on is that it's important to increase your awareness of who you are and where you are right now. Examining every aspect of your life will set you up to take the next step. It will provide you with a stable foundation from which to move forward.

There is no right or wrong way to make a sincere self-evaluation. You don't have to do it perfectly, nor is there a perfect way! The important thing is you make an effort to "Know Thyself".

Now you're ready for the next step, the step that will take you towards the kind of life you have always dreamed about, that wonderful life you really want to be living.

SUMMARY AND ACTION POINTS

- If you want to find out where to go with your life next, you must develop a firm idea of where you stand right now. You need a firm foundation from which to take aim on a new future.

- Remember that you have already created the life you have right now, even if your life is a mess. People create bad situations for themselves because they have not been paying attention to what they are doing with their own thoughts and actions.

- Paying attention to your thoughts and actions will help you gain control over the direction of your life and what you create.

- A fully examined life is a life that is more comprehensively under your control so you can create what you want. This is the ancient wisdom of "Know Thyself".

- Examine every aspect of your life, from the books you read and the movies and television shows you enjoy watching to what you think about from day to day, your hobbies and anything else you think to include.

- Develop a sense of your own "Life Story" as it has played out to date. What has your story been about? What does your story tell you?

- Once you have an idea of where you have come from, having arrived at your present state, you can move forward in a more deliberate manner to create only the outcomes you want in life while ridding yourself of the unwanted aspects.

- You can create the life of your dreams if you figure out what you want then start actively creating that life.

CHAPTER 5

> *"Your imagination creates your intentions and sets your dreams in action"*
>
> (A)LIDA FEHILY

YOU HAVE WHAT IT TAKES TO DISCOVER YOUR LIFE'S WORK

What is your true life's work?

Maybe you have an inkling of your true life's work or maybe you don't have a clue yet what it is but you have a yearning. We all do. If we are not doing what our life's work is supposed to be, we feel an inner longing, an aching desire, a need to find out what we are here on Earth to accomplish. We need to find what is missing.

It can be frustrating if you can't seem to find it. It's actually a good thing when people have this sense of being unfulfilled or a feeling that they are not on the right path. It's good because, at the very least, you have an awareness that there is something else available to you. You most likely want to start your journey as soon as possible – the journey that leads to Being, Doing and Having that which is your perfect niche in life.

I have good news for you: You can draw your life's purpose to you more easily and more quickly than you ever imagined.

You don't have to take any major risks, disrupt your current life, leave your spouse (if you don't want to) or make your children go crazy or feel abandoned. Certainly, sometimes people feel they need a major shake-up or need to take huge risks to get out of their ruts; however, that also tends to come with much greater risks. What I'm saying is that, either way, you can start today trying to find your true life's work – and you can do so without taking a major risk.

If you start with small, simple steps, everything can start changing for you this very day. Your new life can start right now, as soon as you finish this book. You'll find that each tiny movement you make each day brings you just a bit closer to your ultimate dream.

A series of small steps can lead to a life-transforming leap. Those tiny steps add up faster than you think.

It bears repeating: You are closer right now to your ideal life than you ever thought possible.

If you read the previous chapter on taking your life inventory, you have already taken not just a small step but a considerable leap forward. That's because creating your perfect life is about a discovery process. This process leads you deeper into yourself, not in an egotistical way, but in an expanding way in which the ego actually takes a step back. By taking a life inventory, you have set the stage for transformation. You "Know Thyself".

Now you know where you stand, or at least have a better idea of who, what and where you are, and how you got here. From this foundation, you can start building anew. You can start creating what you want.

LOOK WITHIN

Starting with a thorough look within (truly, there is nowhere else where you can really look). An examination of your own past is a reflection of what you have created for yourself. The future answers you seek are not outside yourself either. They are all within as they always have been. The Kingdom of Heaven lies within.

While it is a good thing to obtain help from outside sources such as reading books, learning from others or watching videos that teach you things, in the end it is you who will decide what is best for you.

Only you have the ultimate answers for yourself. You can use the information of other people as helpful guideposts but, in the end, it is you who must shape your own way.

Endeavour to learn to rely on your own inner wisdom to make decisions for yourself.

When you accept the idea that only you are the ultimate authority on your own life, you take responsibility for your own being.

The good thing about that is, the Universe likes this approach. It wants you to be your own, unique self. If you choose to take responsibility for yourself, the Universe will gladly help you along the way. It wants you to take charge. When you do take personal charge of your own life, you receive help from a higher source.

SOLVE YOUR OWN PROBLEMS

You must learn to rely on yourself in difficult life situations.

We can call them "problems" but it helps to reframe these tough situations or problems as "challenges". The fact is, there are no problems if we recognise them for what they are: Opportunities!

Words make a difference. Thoughts matter. Those thoughts you hold in your mind and to which you give frequent verbal expression have a tendency to show up in your daily life.

So often people speak or think this way: "I really need to tackle this problem" or, "I need to solve this problem" or, "I need to get all these troubles behind me so I can move forward" or, "I'm determined to sweep away my misfortunes."

Look at those key words: Problems. Troubles. Misfortunes.

If you keep mentioning these words often enough – guess what? They show up, even if your intention is to talk about removing them from your life.

Rather, say this:

"How can I take on this challenge and make something good come from it?'

   "This is clearly an opportunity for growth."

   "I bet there is a creative solution to this situation."

Frame all your challenges in a *positive* way, both in thoughts and words.

After you assess your situation, it is then up to you to figure out what you are going to do to move forward in love, serenity, joy and happiness. You may choose to do the "right" thing or the "wrong" thing, but the important thing is you begin to take power into yourself.

Keep in mind that perception of "right" and "wrong" is a matter of how you choose to view these events. I'm not saying you'll never make a mistake again. We learn from our mistakes. (In reality, they are not mistakes, they are opportunities!)

What many people have come to call "mistakes" are in fact positive learning experiences. The important thing is that you take responsibility for your own existence. If you make a disastrous decision and mess things up, it's not the end of the world. You have gained a better idea about what not to do. After you make a "mistake", try something else. However, these decisions must be your own and you are obligated to take psychological ownership of them. Again, keep in mind there are never any mistakes in life – just choices.

More often than not, you'll come up with a decent, happy solution. Plus, you'll gain a boost and "feel the power" every time you solve your own "problems" (rather, overcome your own hurdles).

Again, the Universe will recognise that you have finally opted to be a person of power. The Universe wants to help people who are taking the responsibility to make their own personal corner of the Universe a better place.

When you make a commitment to be the builder of your own life, then all the outside influences that often seem to be knocking you backwards will start to lose their power over you.

When you decide your "Locus of Control" resides right there within your own self, you become an authentically powerful individual. You become "empowered".

THINK CREATIVELY

When you take responsibility for facing your own challenges, you automatically begin to think more creatively. For each new challenge you confront, it is natural to want the best outcome. That means you pause and think things through, perhaps to come up with two or three different options for solving a particular dilemma. Coming up with more than one solution challenges you to think creatively.

At first, it may be tough to think creatively on your own, especially if you have been living like a victim or a doormat for a long time. Perhaps you are accustomed to asking someone else what to do. Maybe you're used to following someone else's advice, rather than making your own decisions and accepting responsibility for the consequences which you then perceive as either good or bad.

When you accept the responsibility for yourself, you force yourself to think outside the box. You'll find your ability to become a "creative problem-solver" will start to grow rapidly.

Thinking creatively about how to handle key life situations is like lifting weights to build muscle mass – except results appear much faster than muscles. When you exercise your "creativity muscles", you'll be amazed at how swiftly your deep inner resources – powers you never knew you had – come forth to help you.

At first you solve simple problems – as I said, take baby steps – but with each problem you solve, you gain an ability to take on bigger and bigger challenges. You become more creative, and soon, an incredible power of creativity starts to flow out of you on command – naturally. Remember that "problems" are opportunities for growth and the Universe only gives you as much of these growth experiences as you can handle.

There is no way to see if what I am saying is true until you try it yourself. That's why I urge you to get started right now

– today! Select a small, simple problem you think you have right now and focus on creating a solution, then just go for it! Then do another, and another, and another – and just watch the magic start to happen.

IT'S NOT SELFISH TO FOCUS ON YOURSELF INITIALLY

Many people find themselves forever bogged down in their own problems because they have what I call "martyr syndrome". They are always putting everyone else's problems in front of their own. You may be in a constant state of pushing aside your own housekeeping to help another person with his or her housekeeping. Such people are always helping other people while their own issues fester and become worse. Sometimes that's just the way they like it – to take the focus off solving their own "problems" by keeping busy with everyone else's.

If you think you are in a bad place, you need to stop and consider this for a minute.

Look at it this way:

If a bunch of people fall into a lake, flailing around, trying not to drown, who is in the best position to help them? Yet another person in the lake busily trying not to drown or a person floating in a stable boat or standing on solid ground?

The fact is the person with solid footing is in a much better position to save the others. This person isn't keeping busy trying to stay alive so they are capable of giving the others a hand.

That's the key: You must get yourself into a position of strength FIRST before you can start helping those around you. No, this is not about being selfish and never helping other people – quite the opposite!

You have to help yourself first. What good is it for you to be pulled down to drown along with everyone else?

After you get your own house in order, you'll have plenty of time and opportunities to help others. Remember, other people must learn how to solve their own problems, too, just like you. We can't expect the "local martyr" or someone else to do what we should be doing for ourselves.

Are the constantly needy people you find yourself helping all the time truly growing and learning on their own? Are they thinking creatively or are they always expecting someone else to swoop in and take care of their troubles?

Does it sometimes feel as though everyone around you is sticking a hose into your soul and draining away your energy? Do people stop by while you are busy or need to complete important work only to dump all of their problems on you for an hour or two then leave?

There are certain people I have come to recognise as "psychic vampires". They know you are a "good listener" so they feel they have a right to take up as much of your time as they want in order to vent about their own endless "problems". After they do so, they feel relieved because they have just unloaded all their sorrows onto you. But there you are, more bogged down than ever because you haven't completed any of your own work for the past two hours.

If you find yourself confronted by a lot of psychic vampires, maybe it's time for some tough love. Sometimes you need to let people know that while you do love them, you are busy right now. Everyone needs to take command of their own lives and challenges just as you need to get busy cleaning up your own corner of the Universe. You can take time for other people later, after your own boat has been stabilised.

Get yourself into a position of strength then you can help others as you see fit.

BUSY ALL DAY BUT NOTHING GETS DONE

A lot of people tell me there never seem to be enough hours in the day. From sun up to sun down, they are constantly busy taking care of this chore or that. There's an endless amount of things to do. They rush around, they multitask; they barely finish with one item when another seems to immediately take its place. It's like putting out small brushfires all day. As soon as you stomp out one, another sprouts up.

Yes, you seem to be busy all day. Yet, at the end of the day, it looks like a bomb went off in your living room. The house is a cluttered mess, the dishes still need to be done, the laundry is lying in a heap and you're missing a deadline at work. Yikes! How did it get this way?

Many people think there is no way out of this dilemma.

But there is! All it takes is for you to have a little faith in what I am going to tell you right now. You can free yourself from that "busy hamster running wheel" situation by doing the following:

Simply stop, or at least slow down, and find some quiet time each day so you can visualise your highest priority. That highest priority should be reaching the point in life whereby you are living the life of your dreams, doing what you really want to do. You should have an idea of what this is by now – perhaps you discovered it during your life inventory.

Now, you have decided what you really want to do with your life – what you dream of doing – or at least have a better idea of what you really want to be doing.

Then, take just one step every day that will bring you closer to your dream.

Ignore the busy work for an hour. Let everything else wait until you accomplish your "One Step Towards My Life Dream" task first. After you take that one step, you can go back to the rat-race, busy-work life for the rest of the day – as long as you take time each day to complete one solid action that leads a step closer to your dream life.

That step can be anything. Perhaps you need more information, so take some time to find a book you need or do some research on the Internet which will move you one step closer to your dream goal. Maybe you need to talk to a key person or start teaching yourself a key skill. Whatever you do, you must take that one step each day – and give this step priority over everything else. Let the dishes pile up for an extra hour or leave that pile of laundry for the morning.

You must break the grip that the "busy rat-race" has over you. You do this by taking one step towards your dream life every day.

Remember, the Universe, your Higher Self, or whatever you want to call it, will be helping you.

YOU'RE ALREADY OKAY

You might perceive your life to be a mess right now but you have to remember that this is 100% okay. If you find that everything is a mess, then say, "I bless this mess!" After all, it is only your perception of the situation that is making it look like anything less than perfect. Everything is always as it is, the way it should be in the moment. You can choose the way you think about it.

We are all where we are in the Present Moment for a purpose. It all has meaning. You may not like where you are right now, or even who you are at this instant, but you can still start loving yourself no matter what. Accept yourself and love yourself.

Accept your situation – but don't resign yourself to it.

The Buddhists have a saying: "Acceptance without resignation". This is an excellent attitude to adopt no matter what is happening in your life.

When you accept yourself completely you make it possible to move forward to become the person you envision yourself to be.

Just about everyone is constantly engaged in at least a little self-criticism. We ask ourselves, "Why am I so lazy?" or "Why do I procrastinate so much?" or "Why am I unmotivated?" or "How could I have been so stupid?"

You need to stop that. It's pointless!

Instead, start finding something positive about yourself to admire and feel good about it. Start congratulating yourself for something you do, something you are good at, or some positive trait or strength you have, no matter how small. Focus on it. Give yourself credit where credit is due.

Don't be hard on yourself for your own perceived lack of accomplishments. Start adopting an attitude that is just the opposite; give yourself credit for having survived all you have until this moment. Start acting as your own cheerleader and "life coach".

Develop an inner chatter or dialogue that says:

"I'm doing great!"

"I'm making positive movements forward."

"I'm now on the path to a better life."

"I'm turning things around now."

Say these kinds of things to yourself and about yourself even if you don't believe them.

If you keep it up, you will start believing it. When that happens, expect miracles to follow. What I am suggesting here might sound radically simple but never underestimate the power of developing an inner dialogue of self-encouragement, even self-congratulation.

Don't worry about whether you are just stroking your own ego – because you are probably already doing just the opposite. You are probably busy tearing yourself down little by little, cut by cut, every day. Make it a habit to start doing the opposite. No harm, only good can come from developing an inner pep talk to yourself which becomes a daily habit.

DO THINGS YOU ENJOY EVERY DAY

You must take some time every day to do something you enjoy, no matter how trivial you may think the activity or how much of a time-waster it seems. If you enjoy it, it is not a waste of time. Furthermore, what you truly enjoy doing is maybe a clue to what your true-life purpose really is.

One person to whom I suggested this said: "But what if what I truly enjoy is sitting around and smoking weed?

If you think about this, though, the situation is usually not quite what it seems. Such a person truly may love the feeling of getting high but they might also be beating themselves up about it or they will be sooner or later. The question is, do they really enjoy it in the long run? Even a person who absolutely loves to sit around and get stoned may eventually come to the conclusion that the negative aspects of drugs sooner or later outweigh the "enjoyment" of such an activity.

However, if they don't, they must be prepared to accept the consequences of the choices they've made.

I'm not here to sit in judgement and neither are you.

Again, everyone chooses and creates their own reality. That includes the freedom to make whatever choices they desire. There are no bad choices.

But even a "stoner" has other, more positive things they enjoy besides getting high. Maybe they like to write poetry or build birdhouses. Maybe they like to bake or ride a bicycle. Everyone has something positive they enjoy doing, which they should do as often as possible, whether it seems to have any intrinsic value or not.

Eventually, just doing what you like simply because you enjoy it can be linked to something that might actually make money.

For example, I know a person who loves to read and he discovered he also liked to write book reviews. There was just something about sitting down and telling others what he thought about a particular book that was fun for him. Since he was writing book reviews, he started posting them on a blog, but also put up his reviews on Amazon.com, the biggest bookseller in the world. Amazon encourages all of its customers to submit reviews for whatever they purchase on the site.

Of course, there's no money in writing reviews. It's just a favour you do for others – at least, for five years my book-reviewing friend thought he was doing people a "favour".

After writing more than 230 book reviews, my friend found that his ranking as a reviewer at Amazon had grown very high. Amazon "ranks" reviewers based on how much positive or negative feedback they get from customers. His reviews were well-written, in-depth and helpful, and so it was natural that thousands of Amazon shoppers gave him positive ratings, which in turn gave him "Top Reviewer" status on Amazon.

It didn't take long for product sellers of all kinds to take notice, and not just booksellers. Many companies started requesting my friend to review their products. In exchange, they sent him free samples of that product in exchange for a review – be it a positive or negative review. He began to receive products of all sorts, from electronics and clothing, to kitchen items and pet supplies.

He was obliged to do something with all that free stuff, so he started a side business of selling it, mostly just to local people in his small community. This soon resulted in an extra $500 a month. Suddenly, he was doing what he loved to do and would gladly continue to do it for free, except he was making a lot of extra money on the side.

Stories abound of others who have turned a favourite hobby into a thriving business, some of them worth millions of dollars. A quick search on the Internet will easily find dozens of examples. One woman, for example, turned baking cookies into a multi-million dollar cookie-selling empire.

The point is: Do something you love every day, even if it never earns you a cent. Doing what you love honours your

Inner-Higher Self and draws you closer to fulfilling your true purpose on this planet.

YOU HAVE A SPECIAL TALENT

Many people believe they can never achieve a life of their dreams because they lack the talent or skills to make those dreams come true. This is not true! The very fact that you are here and you exist means you have some kind of special talent, skill or ability that is in some way connected to your larger purpose.

Waking up to your own special talent first requires the belief that you have one, whether you know it right now or not.

Most people spend too much time doubting themselves or decrying the "fact" that they haven't been granted any special gifts. When you catch yourself nursing such doubts or fears, don't fight them; instead, acknowledge them, and then let it go. Try not to worry or berate yourself or struggle against negative self-doubt; rather, try projecting love towards your looming feelings of insecurity and anxiety.

The reason you believe you don't have any natural gifts may be because you have never spent any time searching for them. You just haven't found them yet.

If you think you don't have any natural gifts then make it your goal to discover what they are. That may mean trying new things or taking up an interest in something you may not have considered. **As well as *thinking* outside the box, *do* outside the box.**

Another way to gain a skill or talent you think you might not have is to find someone who does possess that skill or talent – then spend some time with that person. Better yet, find a group of such people and join the associated clubs and professional organisations, try attending meetings or going to seminars. When you hang out with other people who have a high degree of skill in a particular area, those skills may begin to rub off on you. You will be closer to their energy and start to attune and synchronise (resonate) with it. Essentially, you have a kind of psychic absorption from associating with these people.

There is a phenomenon that physicists call "entrainment". It has long been observed that certain objects performing specific functions within the same environment tend to become entrained. For example, if you put 20 grandfather clocks in the same room, all of their pendulums will start swinging in unison with each other, even if they start out of sync with each other. They will become entrained.

Entrainment happens because Mother Nature takes the path of least resistance. Mother Nature likes to make the most efficient use of energy in a given space. It's easier for 20 pendulums to swing together because all of their vibrational sound energy — as carried upon the molecular structure of the atmosphere – supports one another in that immediate environment.

The same effect has been noticed by people who meditate in groups. Experienced meditators say that 10 people all meditating in the room find it far, far easier to go into a deep state than it is for a single person who meditates alone in a private room. Some theorise that the brainwaves of the people resonate with each other. If 20 people in a room all get into a "theta wave" state of brain function, it will be much easier for all of them to stay in that "theta-wave" zone.

The bottom line is, getting involved with those who already have the skills or talents you think you don't have can be an excellent way to gain those abilities for yourself.

HAVE FUN!

If you hate your job, that's a pretty obvious sign you are not fulfilling your purpose. If you truly enjoy your work, you don't have to ask whether you are on the right path or not. If you're enjoying your work and having fun that is the ultimate clue. You are doing what you are supposed to be doing.

You can use the "Am I Having Fun?" test as a way to judge your current situation. If you are not having fun at your work, then search for work that brings you closer to a sense of joy. You know the old saying: "A man who finds a job he loves will never work another day in his life."

Most people only do things that are fun in their spare time such as pursuing a hobby. However, that can be an important clue. Once again, a hobby can eventually be linked to a source of making money, thus becoming your life's work.

Always keep in mind: "It's not always about the money." However, if you find work you love and enjoy, financial issues have a magical way of taking care of themselves.

YOU HAVE WHAT IT TAKES

Rest assured you have what it takes right now to find your life's work. You have what it takes both in your ability to discover unknown skills which you never knew you had and to develop the new skills you need to live your dream life.

Always tell yourself that and repeat it out loud: "I have what it takes."

SUMMARY AND ACTION POINTS

- If you feel you are not living the life you are supposed to live, that's good because this means you have identified a situation you want to improve.

- Drawing your true life's purpose to yourself is far easier than you imagined.

- The answers you seek are never "Out There" but always "Inside Yourself".

- Solve your own problems – don't expect others to solve your problems for you. You must empower yourself by developing the creativity you need to lead you to a better place.

- Strive to break the "Busy All Day" cycle by focusing on your true life purpose and making that a priority.

- It is not selfish to focus on yourself until you reach a high degree of personal self-empowerment.

- Whatever your situation is right now, good or bad, you are "already okay".

- Start doing something you enjoy every day. Start doing it today!

- You have a special talent right now, whether you know it or not.

- "Having fun" is an excellent measure of "right living" for you.

- You have what it takes.

CHAPTER 6

"Miracles happen when you commit to action"

(A)LIDA FEHILY

BELIEF AND ACTION

To live the life of your dreams, you must believe in yourself then take action!

Reading books like the one you have in front of you right now is great but eventually you have to put down all the books and start DOING.

Think about a weight-loss book. Many people read one weight-loss book after another yet they remain overweight. Millions of weight-loss books are sold every year; there are whole bookshelves full of volumes with tips, diets, tricks and methods for losing weight. At the same time, much of the modern Western world is in the midst of an obesity epidemic.

Why aren't all those weight-loss books getting the job done? It's because people are not ACTING on what they learn. There is really only one simple way to lose weight: eat less and exercise more. So why do people need to read 10 or 20 books of 300 pages each to learn something so simple? It's because they tell themselves that reading a book about doing what you want to do is the same as ACTUALLY DOING what you need to do. It's easier to read a book than to run two kilometres every day.

So what you have to do is start taking solid action in the real world – right now, today! In order to make the changes you want, you have to act to live the life of your dreams.

BELIEVE IN YOURSELF

Take a chance on yourself: Believe in yourself!

If you wait for others to start believing in you, or if you wait for those around you to make changes for you, it will never happen. If you expect your new boyfriend or girlfriend, or even your husband or wife, to deliver what you want at your feet, you'll have a long wait. Your spouse may be by your side to support you when you get started but you are the one who must take that first step.

The same goes for your job. Millions of people are waiting for a promotion at work or hoping they will receive a higher salary or a new opportunity. They place their trust outside themselves – in their bosses, the company, the company's future growth potential, the retirement investment plan. They hope for action from all kinds of places associated with their jobs, but rarely from themselves.

No matter who or what it is you're waiting for to make the changes you want, it's likely that nothing much will happen. In your job, for example, if you instead choose to put the responsibility on yourself to become more productive, or you come up with a new idea to help your employer, then you are taking the initiative to start making things happen for yourself.

Some people say to me: "I've tried doing better at work but all that usually happens is my manager gets all the credit" or, "The more work I take on, the more they give me, and I get no reward" or, "Everyone has their place in my office and we're expected to do what we're told."

There are all kinds of reasons and excuses for not advancing at work. In some cases, the situation may indeed be so rigid that there is no opportunity to move to a higher level.

In that case, you can take the initiative to quit that job and find a better employer.

Or you could start your own business and become self-employed so that every task you perform will go toward the betterment of your own life's journey. To start your own business, you need a high degree of belief in yourself. You need to trust yourself. You must be willing to take a risk on yourself. If you don't believe in yourself, you'll never take that leap.

However, you can't wait for someone else to do it for you. For example, some people are willing to start a new business if someone else will "back them" with a financial stake. Sometimes it's a parent or a rich uncle; others appeal to bankers or angel investors. They wait for others to agree to give them the money they think they need before they move forward.

In some cases you must have start-up money – but you can't wait for others to just give it to you. You have to make something happen that will make it worth the risk for others to help you. You have to take action. Or you can find a way to start what they call a "bootstrap business". That means you "pull yourself up by your bootstraps" with no money at all. Millions of people have done it. You start with little or no money then grow as you go. When you earn money, you plunge that back into the business to increase growth.

OTHERS MAY RESIST YOU

One of the biggest roadblocks for people who make a decision to believe in themselves is the people around them. If you plan to take risks to make changes, often people will immediately raise objections or criticise your new initiative even once you have stepped onto your new path.

They will also warn you about risks and dangers and tell stories about some other person who tried the same thing and was met with disaster. Many people will say, "Play it safe. Your situation is not so bad right now."

You might hear dozens of statements like these from people who are close to you.

Even a loving and supportive spouse can be the first to come up with a reason why you should not embark on your new life plan. That's understandable since they probably have both an emotional and financial stake in what you do. However, even when resistance is coming from someone as close as your own intimate partner, your challenge is to endeavour to honour your own soul.

If you are holding yourself back to please a spouse, your friends, your boss, your children, you are not really doing them any favours. Most of all, you are not doing yourself a favour. These people are around you because of the Law of Reflection – they reflect the self-doubt within yourself. Once you believe in yourself, the people around you will reflect that as well.

By denying the central purpose of your own soul, you are also denying yourself the ability to be the best wife, husband, father, mother, friend, etc that you can be to those around you.

CREATE AND FOLLOW YOUR OWN SELF-IMAGE

A lot of people spend their whole lives adopting and fulfilling an image someone else has created for them. Most often this is a parent insisting that a child take up a certain profession or career path.

History is filled with examples of people whose parents wanted them to go to law school, business school or medical school but the child rebelled and took up music or the arts – and became rich and famous in the process.

When you create your own self-image based on your inner impulses and heart's desire, you are coming from an authentic place that honours who you are and who you were meant to be. Then, when you achieve success, you owe that success to no one but yourself. If you fail miserably – well, yes, you will have to own that, too. However, failure is often a part of the journey.

At the risk of using a cliché: "We learn from our mistakes." It's a cliché but it's accurate, other than that they are not really "mistakes" but opportunities for learning and change.

In fact, "failure" is often necessary. That's because recovering from perceived failure is what makes us stronger. It is said that when we break a bone in our body, after it heals it becomes even stronger than it was before. Sometimes we work through a series of "failures" so that when we finally get to where we want to be, we can really appreciate the wonderful place we have finally created for ourselves.

Then we sit back and laugh at all of our "screw-ups". Of course, there really are no screw-ups, only different choices that lead in new directions of growth. They only seem to be screw-ups at the time and that's because we choose to perceive them that way.

THERE IS SOMETHING BETTER

You must not only believe in yourself to manifest the life you want, but you have to believe that a different life for yourself is possible.

You have to believe that a better situation is waiting for you, if you can take the steps to achieve it.

No matter how deep and miserable your current rut is (or you believe it to be), you must believe that change is possible. You must absolutely accept that a different way of life can be achieved, even if you don't know what that is yet.

In an earlier chapter I asked you to conduct a life review and to take on the task of getting to "Know Thyself". If you did that, you may have already figured out just what it is you want to do, or you might at least have some clues as to the direction you can start moving toward.

However, others still may have no idea of where to go next. They desperately want to change their lives, to get out of whatever boring or even miserable situation they are in right now – and yet, they just can't figure out what change to make. It's true that some people have no idea what their own "ultimate dream life" even is.

If that's you, then just start somewhere. Take out a clean sheet of paper right now and list three situations that would be better than your current situation. Maybe that means working in a different job or living in a different location. It might mean you finally declutter your house or you dedicate yourself to losing 20 kilos. It could be anything.

Let your mind go free to brainstorm different situations. You never know when your subconscious mind will suddenly jump forward, grab your hand and write down something that will amaze you. It's almost as if your hand did the writing on its own.

Whatever the case, start believing right now that a different life does exist for you and you can get yourself to that new life – and start living it.

YOU'RE NOT TOO OLD

One of the biggest excuses I hear from many of my clients who are unhappy in their current situation is that they are "too old to change now".

This is 100% untrue. I have a close friend who started writing novels at age 60 and he had never written a word before. His first novel was accepted by a small publisher and sold well. It wasn't an international bestseller but he found a small cult following of readers who loved his book. This inspired him to write a second novel, a third, and he is currently working on his fourth.

He sells enough books to make money, but the greater joy for him is that he has a following of fans who send him kind letters of praise and they keep encouraging him to "write another book". He gets invited to paid speaking engagements and to lecture at libraries and book clubs.

At age 60, he started a whole new life.

Or consider a Texan woman by the name of Helen Small. In 2010, she earned her master's degree in psychology from the University of Texas in Dallas. She was 90 years old on her graduation day.

Helen first entered college in 1939 but left college at the insistence of her new husband who wanted her to stay home to be a wife and mother. That's generally the way things were done in the late 1930s and women rarely questioned it. The men were the "breadwinners" and the women stayed home to keep the home fires burning, rear the children, and have supper ready on the table when their men came home from a hard day's work.

In 2004, Helen, now a grandmother, was determined to finish the college degree she had put on hold 65 years previously. Her children had been raised and had since grown up and gone off on their own. She was no longer "just a housewife" for her husband. Yet, getting back into the modern world was far from easy. She had a lot of catching up to do. For example, she had to get up to speed with computers, the Internet and delve into long study sessions to gain the background information she needed across a variety of subjects.

It was her dream to not only finish college but to further her studies for an advanced degree. At age 90, she was awarded her master's degree, and she became a role model for thousands of people.

How about Mary Moe of Washington D.C.? At age 91, she earned her private pilot's license, fulfilling a dream she had developed some 80 years earlier when as a child she had become inspired by famous pilots Charles Lindbergh and Amelia Earhart.

Like many women of the 1930s, Moe had to put her dream of flying on hold for a variety of reasons – for marriage, raising a family and work. She even fought a deadly bout with breast cancer – a battle she eventually won.

Finally, in the year 2014 at age 91, Mary Moe decided it was high time she learned to fly – a dream she had never abandoned over nearly a century of life. With the help of a local charitable organisation, Moe strapped herself into the seat of a single-engine Cessna next to a flight instructor and, several lessons later, made her first solo flight. She had earned her private pilot's licence.

Mary told a local newspaper reporter: "I got a few tears while I was up there ... I couldn't believe it was finally happening ... I wish I'd done this 50 years ago."

One could write an entire book about people who take on new challenges in their sixties, seventies, eighties and nineties. What's amazing is that I hear people all the time in their thirties, forties and fifties, who say: "I'm too old to chase my dreams now. My best years are already behind me."

What nonsense!

You're never too old to start an all-new life. Millions of people have done it and continue to do it every day.

DEVELOP YOUR HIGHER SKILLS AND GET TO WORK

The examples of my novelist friend, master's graduate Helen Small and pilot Mary Moe show we will benefit from taking the time and using the energy to develop the right skills to help us realise our dreams.

A lot of people feel they are being held back or that they are stuck in the same old rut. They have come to believe that because they lack the skills they can't access the lives of their dreams. The obvious answer to this problem is to start believing in yourself, get busy and acquire the skills you require. Developing these skills is not only part of the journey, but part of the fun!

My novelist friend had never written a word before age 60 but he worked hard to remedy his lack of literary skills. For example, he subscribed to *Writer's Digest* magazine and read it cover to cover every month. He read books on how to plot a novel and how to create believable characters. He took some creative writing night courses at a local community college. Most of all, he sat down and started writing something every day, even before he truly knew what he was doing.

Just "DOING SOMETHING" can be magical. When you decide to believe in yourself, take action to help yourself and ignore any naysayer criticism you get along the way; there is no limit to where you can go and what you can do.

SUMMARY AND ACTION POINTS

- Start believing in yourself – today!

- Develop the belief that something better exists for you right now.

- Create your own self-image and follow it. Never let others develop it for you.

- Start doing something right now, at least one step per day; that step moves you towards a new lifestyle. Focus on your fondest dreams and start taking specific steps to make those dreams come true.

- Learn to resist and ignore those around you who doubt you or try to drag you down. Never listen to the criticism of others. They don't know what's best for you. Only you know what is best for you. Remember, the people around you tend to reflect your own self-doubt. That means they will also reflect your own positive beliefs in yourself.

- You are never too old to make a major change in your life.

- Always remember: You must always be DOING SOMETHING to move TOWARDS YOUR DREAM – every day.

CHAPTER 7

> *"Gratitude is the key to life —
> it opens up all the doors"*
>
> Ⓐ LIDA FEIHLY

THE POWER OF GRATITUDE

The most powerful force in the Universe is love, but some say there is one other "force" that may be a close second. This force is that feeling we experience as "gratitude". You might also define it as "the joy of appreciation of what is".

What is gratitude, really? It doesn't seem to be purely an emotion, yet it is something we feel. On the other hand, we employ our mind or intellect to appreciate gratitude. However, gratitude clearly is more than just an intellectual concept.

Gratitude seems a hybrid creature that is part intellectual recognition of a something or a situation combined with a sense of contentment and feelings of joy. Furthermore, this intellectual-emotional response can be trained to focus on anything we choose – be it good or bad. What's amazing is that if you are not so good at feeling gratitude, this response can be learned.

Those who have made in-depth, statistical studies of the process of manifesting (yes, such studies have been done) noticed that those people who seem to have the most success at manifesting the things they want in life also tend to nurture a sense of gratitude for everything they receive.

They also seem to be grateful for even those areas of their lives that are not so bright. For example, they're the kind of people who take a look at their house on a day when every room looks like a pigsty, yet they say, "Bless this mess!"

If they don't naturally have feelings of acceptance for their messy house, they consciously work to conjure such feelings, then go with them. They accept it but they don't resign themselves to it. Then they can either clean up the house with a sense of joy and energy or they can say, "The heck with it. I'm going to watch a movie and I'll tidy up later. The dishes will still be there in a couple of hours."

They feel happy and grateful either way.

I also like what long-time self-help author Melody Beattie wrote about gratitude:

"Gratitude unlocks the fullness of life. It turns what we have into enough, and more. It turns denial into acceptance, chaos to order, confusion to clarity. It can turn a meal into a feast, a house into a home, a stranger into a friend."

Gratitude also is a recognition that true joy originates from within ourselves and is not dependent on anything external. For example, maybe the only good thing you have to eat today are some dried up leftovers in your refrigerator. You're short on cash so you can't go to the market for at least a couple more days. Thus, it's either eat the leftovers you have right now or go hungry.

By learning to nurture a feeling of gratitude toward any situation we confront, we can easily turn a warmed-over plate of leftovers into a fabulous feast. We can say or think to ourselves: "I'm incredibly lucky to have something to eat today."

I warn you to stop that sentence right there and don't follow on to think the typical stereotype of: "I know that millions of other people are going hungry and not as lucky as I am right now."

This second part, while acknowledging that others are less fortunate than you, may not be a good habit to start. So rather than thinking, "Well, at least I'm not as bad off as (fill in the blank)", always frame your thoughts and words entirely in the positive.

This doesn't mean you don't care about others who are less fortunate. It's just that, in shaping your own world, your own primary reality and your own personal environment, you want to always keep everything as positive as possible.

What if you don't actually and truly feel grateful for a cold plate of leftovers? Well, there's that old saying: "Fake it till you make it." Others phrase it as "Act as if"... That means if you don't truly feel gratitude in your heart for a dried up plate of noodles, just "act as if" you are grateful. Sooner or later, and if you keep doing it enough, your heart will follow your mind.

The great English poet and artist William Blake (1757–1827) said, "Gratefulness is heaven itself."

He was right about that.

An "attitude of gratitude" has long been recommended by wise men, shamans, ancient teachers and now our modern-day psychologists. Getting yourself into a feeling of gratitude changes the very vibrational level of your entire being – your mind, body and spirit.

The amazing thing about gratitude is that it seems to work both backward and forward in time. That means that if you strive to make yourself grateful for something you don't have today, you can make it far more likely you will obtain that thing or situation in the future. It's as if a feeling of gratitude can reach into the future to set up a target point and draw you towards the completion of what you visualised earlier. You complete the cycle you set in motion in the past.

This works hand-in-hand with the practice of visualisation. Many high achievers have learned that one of the best ways to bring about a desired situation is to visualise that situation as powerfully and clearly as you can. You get yourself into a quiet, perhaps meditative state, and build a powerful "inner vision" of what it is you want to draw to yourself.

Then you imagine you already have it – and you feel incredibly grateful for it. This unleashes incredible power – your very own power to manifest exactly what you want and to shape your corner of the Universe according to your direct will and intention.

Your subconscious mind also participates. As I have said, the subconscious mind does not know the difference between the truth and a lie. But perhaps it is better to say, the subconscious mind does not know the difference between something that is real and unreal. It does not know that what you are visualising right now, in the Present Moment, has not yet come to pass – it's something you want to appear in your life. If you visualise it strongly enough, then feel grateful for it, you will energise your subconscious mind into doing everything it can to bring about what you want. If you act as if you already have it, the effect is even stronger.

Thus, we see that gratitude works in many and varied ways, as well as in cooperation with other aspects of our make-up and "psychic tools" as human beings.

It's important to be grateful for the "small things" as well as "big things." For example, let's say you only have a small amount of money. Most people consider this to be a primary source of misery or "lack" in their lives. Every time they go out to spend their small amount of money, they feel troubled by it, or even miserable.

The thought process goes something like this:

> *"I only have $20 and I need to go to the grocery store to buy some food. God, I hate it when I need so many things but only have $20! It's always so difficult to figure out what to buy and what I have to do without. I have to make sure I get only the essentials. That means I have to pass on all of those things that I like so much. I really wish I could just go to the grocery store and*

throw anything I want into my shopping cart, even if it's something I don't absolutely need, like potato chips or cookies. Unfortunately, I can't splurge on things like that – I just have to get the basics, like milk and butter, then find a way to make everything stretch. I just don't like being so limited with the basic things in life, like food."

I bet this sounds familiar to a lot of people. Probably just about all of us have been in that position at one time or another. Some people say it is just being "realistic" to have thoughts like these – after all, if you only have enough money to buy the basic things you need, you don't have the extra money, right?

Well, no, that's not exactly right. The fact is, it is this very nurturing of thoughts and feelings of scarcity and limitations that keeps you mired in that same situation– until you learn to change the way you think.

The fact is if you feel troubled and insecure about spending small amounts of money, you will also have the same problem if you have large amounts of money.

Every time you resent paying a bill, every time you have feelings of insecurity when you purchase an item – no matter how small – and every time you feel anxiety about running out of money in the near future, you reinforce that condition of not having enough money.

The cure is to consciously start nurturing the opposite feelings and attitudes. For example, you may absolutely hate to pay your electricity bill, or your rent, or your car insurance bill. When you submit your payment you may be feeling resentment and even a small amount of fear. You remind yourself you are living "pay cheque to pay cheque" and you can barely afford the car insurance bill.

As difficult as it might seem, try to change the way you feel and think about each bill you pay, no matter how hard it is.

When you pay your rent, or submit the payment for your electricity bill using your online payment account, tell yourself: "I am so absolutely grateful that I have the money to pay my bills. It feels great to take care of this bill! I am so happy to have the electricity I get in return for my money."

The fact is the Universe may be waiting for you to alter your feelings about small amounts of money before it allows you to have large amounts of money.

If a person is constantly fretting, complaining and worrying over small amounts of money, the Universe may think something like: "This person clearly has a problem with money. Imagine the trouble they could get into with a large amount of money."

Indeed, this scenario has been played out dozens of times in real life. In particular, I'm talking about people who have won millions, even tens of millions of dollars in a lottery. A study conducted of lottery winners found that 9 out of 10 of them wished they had never obtained such an incredible amount of cash. In fact, a sudden extremely large windfall of money can ruin lives faster than just about anything else.

I won't go into great detail here but learning about what happens to lottery winners should be required reading for everyone who dreams of winning the "Big One". In case after case, the result of suddenly obtaining millions of dollars very rapidly results in family strife, arguments and splits between family members. In fact, most lottery winners find that they have to move away from their homes, often to another city, where no one knows them or can find them – including their own closest relatives.

Other lottery winners have ended up in extremely difficult situations or their fortunes have wreaked havoc on the lives of loved ones. Still others find that they blow through their winnings in just a few years – even if it is tens of millions of dollars – and, amazingly, many of them end up not only broke but deeper in debt than they ever were before.

A classic example is a British man by the name of Michael Carroll. He was just 19 years old when he cashed in big with a lottery ticket winning £9.7 million (US$14.5 million or AUD$20.3 million). The year was 2002.

He was set for life, except that he wasn't. It took him 10 years but by 2012, he was not only flat broke but in debt. He was also in a lot of legal trouble brought on by his drug-fuelled, wild lifestyle. His winnings caused him to take on this extravagant existence, much of it self-destructive, which included not only drugs but prostitutes, wild parties, fast cars and the purchase of a mansion which turned into "party central".

After the dust had settled, Michael Carroll landed a job working at a menial job in a biscuit factory in Scotland. (Biscuits are "cookies" in the US.) Now he earns about £300 (US$450 or AUD$630) per pay period – and guess what? He says he has never been happier. He's glad the nightmare is over. Now he can enjoy a simple, honest life, and he even feels as though he has more money now than he did before.

Wait a minute: With these scary stories about the lottery, am I not planting negative feelings or fears about money, especially about large amounts of money, in your head?

Well, first of all, I can't make you think or do anything. You are in charge of your own life and destiny. No one is a "victim" of what they read, hear or watch on TV or see anywhere else.

Second, we all must develop a more mature perspective when it comes to the subject of money. Too many people think that the answer to all their problems is having piles of cash. Thus, they can never develop a sense of gratitude in those times when money seems to be an agonising persistent problem in their lives.

The bottom line is: When we learn to be grateful for what we have right now, no matter what it is, even small amounts of money, then that gratitude causes magical things to start happening for us.

When you develop a sense of gratitude for the spare change in your pocket, even when that's about all you have, you'll find that gratitude tends to draw more money to you. You'll find you have just the right amount that will make you happy, and it is in balance with the rest of your life.

Receiving too much money all at once can cause as many, if not more, problems than not having enough money. The key is to be grateful for what you have right now. By that, I mean truly, genuinely grateful. Just do that, then sit back and let the magic happen – it will.

Nurturing feelings of gratitude causes significant shifts to occur in your conscious and subconscious minds. This will accelerate your path towards growth and success much more than doing merely the physical work without the feelings of "positivity". All your hard work is pointless if you have the wrong attitude. Gratitude is the path of least resistance. Its power is superior to "hard work" – yes, the same "hard work" that people often remind you that you need to undertake to have a successful life.

Learning to be grateful for things and situations you don't like is really a turbo-booster that leads you towards everything you love about life. However, you have to love where you are first, no matter how dismal your situation seems to be right now. Against all odds and common sense, strive to be joyful, happy, appreciative and grateful for where you are in this moment. You are alive and you have a purpose. You never have to remain "stuck" in any one place.

Accepting undesirable conditions in your life means you acknowledge that whatever happens to you is for the highest good – but remember nothing ever "just happens" to you. Rather, you create everything; you draw all conditions of life to yourself with your thoughts, words, actions and feelings.

To borrow a famous phrase from the cult TV show and movie franchise Star Trek: "Resistance is futile." Resisting unwanted conditions with bitterness, fretting and anxiety only makes these situations stickier, like flypaper, or quicksand.

The more you struggle and resist, the more you become mired in your unhappy condition. The solution is to *accept* and feel *gratitude* for where you are right now and know that your path leads ever forward, outward and upward. Get excited about the fact you will soon be moving on. Engaging gratitude loosens the grip of resistance.

On a soul level, we all have constant gratitude for all aspects of existence. Your soul knows it is immortal. It knows that whatever negative experience you have in any given moment is not only temporary but a highly valuable learning experience. When you feel gratitude in challenging situations, you strengthen the connection between yourself and your Soul Self.

Feelings of gratitude will ignite your soul because it strengthens the bond between your manifesting mind and your Higher Self, Soul or whatever you want to call it. When you start 'feeding' your soul gratitude, it responds in kind by helping you manifest what you want to manifest.

You can be confident that gratitude always makes a direct connection to what it is directed towards. If you feel gratitude for whatever amount of money you have right now, you send more energy towards your money-manifesting ability.

Of course, gratitude is not all about money. It's about everything. There is definitely a spiritual dimension to gratitude but it is oh-so-practical too. It helps you get things done – or, more accurately – it builds a foundation to help guide you towards exactly the right kind of prosperity and success you have dreamed of in all aspects of life.

SUMMARY AND ACTION POINTS

- Gratitude is one of the most powerful "forces" in the Universe.

- If you don't have genuine feelings of gratitude for being alive and where you are today, you can nurture these feelings and practice having a sense of gratitude in order to make it real in your life.

- It is extremely important to experience gratitude for the small things as well as the big things.

- Gratitude strengthens the connection between your Earthbound physical self and your Soul Self.

- Gratitude creates future targets of success then draws you to them.

CHAPTER 8

> *"Your reality will reflect your feelings as they resonate with the people, places and events around you"*
>
> (A)LIDA FEHILY

EMOTIONS AND FEELINGS

Have you ever been having a normal day when, all of a sudden, you start feeling very depressed?

Just a minute ago, you were feeling normal or even quite cheerful, then a gloom descends upon you, seemingly out of nowhere. Everyone experiences this from time to time; for others, it's an all-too-often event.

Yes, some people are depressed all the time but that's not what I'm talking about. I'm talking about those inexplicable sudden rushes of emotion that can creep up from nowhere and grip you suddenly. This can be true for negative emotions like depression but also for just the opposite.

Suddenly, for no specific reason, you just start feeling light-hearted and joyful.

If you have noticed, I have been using two different terms: "feelings" and "emotions". Maybe you have always thought that these were one and the same; that they were interchangeable terms.

Well, they're not. Knowing the difference between a "feeling" and an "emotion" can make a huge difference in how you perceive the world. Knowing the difference can also provide you with a tremendous resource, a powerful tool that will enable you to gain control of your life, your mind and your total reality. It's also important for leveraging your ability to manifest what you want to bring into your life.

So let's first define our terms, starting with emotions.

According to psychologists, emotions are biological and organic. They are not "mental" events so much as they are biological reactions stored in your body that have a lot more to do with basic brain and body chemistry than they do your conscious, rational mind. That's right: Emotions are technically irrational, be they good or bad.

Now when I say that emotions are "irrational" I don't mean in a negative way. That's because there are both positive and negative emotions. Emotions only become "positive" or "negative" when we start thinking about them and making value judgements about them. When we start thinking about them, they become "feelings".

So what are feelings?

Human beings form feelings in the part of the brain that is

awake and thinking rationally about the world. This takes place in the brain's neocortex, the source of higher thought, as opposed to those regions of the brain that are handling your basic body functions such as regulating your liver or keeping your heart pumping.

When you experience emotions from the deeper, biological part of your brain-body, your rational mind starts forming an opinion about them. It starts to categorise and judge them and even define them. That is a "feeling". You are interpreting what the emotions of your body seem to be telling you. Feelings are influenced by your personal experience, your belief system and your memory.

In short, you have direct control over your feelings; you do not control your emotions – that is, until you decide how you feel about them. You can choose how you want to feel about an emotion then you can take action to either degrade or enhance that emotion.

Again, just to be clear:

Emotions are creatures of the body.

Feelings are creatures of the mind.

HOW DOES KNOWING THIS HELP YOU?

Knowing the difference between feelings and emotions can clear up a lot of confusion in your life. It can also give you much more direct control over how you react to difficult challenges, or respond to happy events.

Too many people are slaves to their emotions. A sense of sadness or depression suddenly arises in you and you don't know why. You think you have no choice but to give in and feel depressed. Maybe you just decide to stay in bed or sit at your kitchen table and cry while life flows on around you.

But where did that feeling of depression come from? And do you have to be a victim of it?

The answer is clearly: "NO!"

That's because you have a choice about how you THINK about that sense of depression or sadness or fear. Yes, you can choose how to FEEL about what your biological body is telling you. You can CHANGE the way you feel about a sudden onslaught of depression and literally drain it away from your mind.

Understanding is the key.

Let me give you an example. A very good friend of mine, whom I'll call Phillipa, told me about a time when she was just having a normal day shopping in the grocery store then something very odd happened.

She was walking down the aisle where they kept the cookies. She was in an entirely routine mode, just shopping, when her eyes spotted a kind of shortbread cookie they call "Windmill Cookies". They are shaped like those old-fashioned Dutch windmills.

There was just something about those cookies. It was almost as if she became fixated upon them. She stopped, picked up a cookie packet and pondered them for a moment.

Suddenly, a terrific sense of gloom and sadness arose within her – but it went beyond that. Standing there in the cookie aisle, Phillipa felt an inexplicable sensation of hopelessness. It was a bright sunny day outside and the interior of the supermarket had seemed so cheerful just a minute before. Phillipa felt she couldn't even finish her shopping. She just walked away from her half-filled cart and drove home. Finally home, she sat down and cried softly to herself.

She could think of absolutely no reason why she was so sad. All in all, her life was going along just fine. In fact, she was just starting to enjoy the success of her self-starter business. About five years previously she had quit her day job to create her own video production company. After a few years of struggle and striving to make ends meet, Phillipa's cash flow was kicking into high gear. She was doing what she loved. She was her own boss, made her own hours and was becoming financially successful. Her personal relationships were great. She had a boyfriend and everything was going well with him. She had friends, hobbies and an interesting social life.

Yet, a simple trip to the grocery store and fixating on a package of cookies had sent her into a gloom that lasted for the rest of the week. She just couldn't shake it – and she could not explain it. It all seemed so inexplicable.

To cut a long story short: After several more weeks of an ongoing struggle with a sense of gloom and despair she could not cast off, Philippa sought the help of a psychiatrist. Her psychiatrist wanted to put her on antidepressant medication which she refused. She just didn't want to go down that road. She didn't want to become dependent on an artificial "chemical fix" no matter how safe the drug was proclaimed to be, especially as she had read reports that long-term use can be harmful. After a month of talk therapy, which didn't seem to be working, her psychiatrist decided to hypnotise her.

Philippa was an excellent subject for hypnotherapy and went under easily. Her psychiatrist regressed her backwards in time, down through the avenues of her mind, instructing her to find the source of her black mood.

It turns out that Philippa was an adopted child. Of course, this was nothing new to her, but there was something that occurred early in her life as a toddler that she had totally forgotten about. When she was still a baby, her father had abandoned her and her mother had developed severe alcoholism. At age three, Philippa had been taken away from her mother by social services and placed in a foster home.

Unfortunately, Philippa's foster parents did not take her in permanently because they were having financial struggles. The main reason they took in foster children was because it involved receiving a certain amount of financial support from the foster care agency.

Under hypnosis, Philippa recalled being hungry all the time. Her foster parents had little time for her: keeping her in a cold room, mostly alone, ignoring her basic needs for much of the day including not giving her enough to eat. In fact, Philippa recalled that, for days on end, she was provided only one thing to eat: shortbread "Windmill Cookies".

Philippa was eventually placed with another caretaker then formally adopted by two wonderful parents who raised her with love and kindness. As the years passed, her sad, lonely and hungry experience as a three-year-old faded from her memory.

Suddenly, 35 years later, a chance encounter with a package of cookies in a grocery store nearly dismantled her normal, happy life.

This is a classic example of an "emotion" rising up, seemingly from "nowhere". However, it didn't just appear from nowhere. Philippa's experience of being hungry and abandoned had been fixed in her biological brain to be associated with emotions of sadness and loneliness. It was so early in her life, her conscious memory of it was forgotten but her brain and body didn't forget. The biological chemical combination of that tragic situation was still within her, lurking there, just waiting to be triggered by a chance association she confronted in her present day.

When those emotions accosted her, she could not understand why she was "feeling" that way. But once she understood the source of the emotion, she could then change the way she "felt" about it. This means that Philippa was not a victim to her own inner sensations.

Now that she understands the source of her inexplicable despair, she can say to herself:

> *"I'm not in that situation anymore. Everything happens for a reason. Yes, that was a sad time in my early childhood, but I survived it, which shows*

how strong and resilient I am. It was all part of my experience of life. Experiencing sadness, hunger and abandonment has made me more compassionate towards others today. That's because I understand what it is like to 'be there'. Now I can turn around and show empathy and understanding for others who have experienced hunger and loneliness."

Everything happens for a reason. Life is a journey. The more awareness and understanding we obtain from our Inner Selves, the more direct power we acquire to start shaping and directing our journey. We can become the captain of our own ship and point our vessel in the direction we want to go, moving towards our highest purpose and potential.

EMOTIONS ARE LIKE BATTERIES

Here is another interesting aspect of emotions that will help you understand them and, thus, enable you to better know yourself and deal with what you sense happening inside your mind and body.

Many psychologists have compared "emotions" to "energy". Anger is energy. Love is energy. Depression is energy. Joy is energy.

This "emotional" energy is stored in our bodies, not just our brains. There is good evidence that we all "feel" or experience emotion throughout our bodies. Emotions are energies that are stored in every cell, brain chemical and possibly all biological tissues (as far as we know). That should come as no surprise to anyone. We have all felt "butterflies in our stomachs" when we are excited, afraid or experiencing thrilling emotions. We sometimes feel "pain in our hearts".

Okay, so what can we do with this self-knowledge? The key word here is "energy". As we all know, energy is not only stored – as in a battery – but energy can be both "charged" and "discharged".

The thing about energy is that it is always changing. In general, energy tends to go from a high state to a low state. For example, the energy stored in your flashlight batteries will eventually run down, so you either buy a new battery or recharge the ones you have if they're rechargeable.

All life on Earth would end if there was no more energy radiating into our planet's biosystems. The Earth's energy comes from the Sun. All life on Earth is made possible because the Sun is constantly "charging" or adding energy to our world. A plant is an energy absorber. Plants convert sunlight into energy which they use to build their cells, stems, leaves and fruits. We then take that plant-created energy and put it into our own bodies by eating the plants. If the Sun died, or our atmosphere was covered by thick UV-blocking clouds, the energy on the surface of the planet would also die.

You can think of the energy of emotions in the same way. Understanding how this works will help you cope with "bad" emotions and allow you to nurture "good" ones.

For example, let's say a person is experiencing sadness for some reason. Sadness is energy but, like energy, it can be discharged. Once the energy of sadness is discharged, it's gone – or at least reduced to a tolerable level. As long as sadness does not become "charged up" again, it will remain at an unnoticeable level.

So one way to get rid of a sad feeling is to just "sit with it" and let yourself experience it, perhaps in a meditative or contemplative state. Just let it flow and let it discharge. Believe me, a feeling of sadness cannot last forever if you mindfully allow it to just flow through your consciousness.

Again, think of the source of that sadness as being like a battery. It only has a limited capacity. It simply can't "run" forever. Sooner or later, you will deplete the energy reserve of that sadness and it will go away – or at least be greatly reduced.

The key is to not let your thinking "busy mind" interfere with the process. When I say you should "sit with an emotion" it is important to understand that this means to "sit without thinking about it" as you don't want to "feed" it more energy. You only want to experience the emotion; be with it. Do not start forming opinions about it, judging it, worrying about it, trying to explain it, justifying it or most importantly struggling against it.

If you struggle against an emotion, you tend to recharge and bolster its energy. No, you just want to let it flow, in one direction, so to speak, until it discharges. This is especially true of all those sad or negative emotions that bother you, limit you or make your life miserable in any way. Always remember that the energy of negative emotions has a limited capacity so you can let them run into the ground.

True, many people experience ongoing emotions they just can't seem to get rid of, even if they mindfully attempt to discharge them. That's because something in their minds is actually working to replenish the battery of that unwanted emotion, or store it, so they don't understand where it is coming from, as was the case with my friend, Philippa.

It all comes back to what I was talking about in Chapter 4: "Know Thyself". The more you understand your own mind, how it works, how you formed an opinion about something, how you came to "feel" a certain way, or where an emotion was created, the more ability you have to shape your entire consciousness in a directed way – in a way that leads to what you truly want for yourself.

Sometimes it helps to find the source of an emotional energy, as Philippa's did. Once she knew what was causing her depression, she could then work on "discharging" that energy, especially because she knew she no longer had to be controlled or influenced by it. But even if she had not learned about the ultimate origin of her sudden malaise, she still could have taken steps to discharge its energy.

Although the basic premise of what I'm talking about is simple, I realise it can seem very complicated.

For example, psychologists tell us that emotions often remain stubbornly "unconscious" through the process of "repression" and also "self-deception". However, I'm not going to go any further down this rabbit hole because I'm not a trained psychologist. I'll let the professionals handle things like "repression" and "self-deception". I don't want to become tangled in a lot of professional, medical jargon. My goal here is to give you some idea about the fundamental workings of the mind, along with the important difference between emotions and feelings.

The fact that you are the one who chooses and directs your feelings can be a source of great power for you. It means you do not have to be a slave to painful emotions, even if you don't necessarily understand where those emotions are coming from.

Knowledge is power!

When you know this, you can change the way you think about emotions and have a much greater ability to chart your own course throughout life.

EBB AND FLOW

Finally, remember that all energy has a natural flow. It ebbs and flows. Energy is in a constant process of moving from a high state to a low state and then back again. Sometimes, when we are on a high, we feel as though it will last forever. The same can be true for when we are feeling low. Too often, when a person is depressed, they think that something major is wrong and they can't seem to see the light at the end of the tunnel, feeling as though their depression is a long-term situation. Then they start to struggle against it, which only makes it worse.

Energy comes and energy goes. Most of the time, all we have to do is wait around for a while and things change. You can always depend on change. In fact, some people say that the only certainty in life is that things will change.

When it comes to emotions, we have to learn to live gracefully with a certain amount of uncertainty. There are clearly times when you need to take action if your mental condition seems to be settling in for the long term and starts disrupting your life.

One thing is certain: You have far more control over the way you feel and think than you may have realised. The more you get to know your Inner Self and the more you foster a deeper understanding of your psyche, the better you will become at leading a joyful life. With true Inner Knowledge on your side, a positive life is far more likely to occur than a negative.

Please note: I acknowledge I have only touched on what can be a rather complex topic which can also, unfortunately, be confused and muddled by all kinds of psychological theories.

Simply knowing about the difference between emotions and feelings provides you with one more powerful tool to help you move your life in the direction you want, towards the life of your dreams.

Remember that one of the greatest keys to manifesting what you want in life is to visualise your dreams; feel as if you already have your dream life and act as if it's real; visualise having your dreams come true and how that feels. Through The Law of Reflection it will present in your reality.

SUMMARY AND ACTION POINTS

- Emotions and feelings are not the same.

- Emotions are biological and non-rational.

- Feelings are rational and generated by your higher, or thinking, mind.

- You can change the way you "feel" about "emotions".

- Emotions carry energy. Energy can be charged and discharged.

- All forms of energy naturally ebb and flow in a constant cycle of change.

- No one need ever be a slave to their emotions.

- You can learn to "charge up" and nurture positive emotions and "discharge" and eliminate negative emotions.

- When it comes to both feelings and emotions, it's best to always accept a certain amount of uncertainty with grace and patience.

CONCLUSION

"You have the power and wisdom to create abundance in your life"

Ⓐ LIDA FEHILY

Today, more than ever, we have become a people addicted to immediate outcomes. We want everything to happen fast, "right now"! Our culture has been trending this way for a long time but with the advent of the Internet, our desire of immediate gratification for so many things seems to have been magnified.

When we surf the net, we want the information we are searching for to come to us at lightning speed. If a web page takes too long to load, it's CLICK OFF and move immediately to some other online location where you expect things to pop up faster.

When we shop online, we demand fast two-day shipping or, better yet, overnight shipping. Online retailers are well aware that the short delay between buying a product and having that product in hand is the primary roadblock to making more sales. That's why giants like Amazon.com and Wal-

Mart are now experimenting with delivery by aerial drone in a "what will they think of next?" drive to beat competitors. They are desperate to get consumer "goods" to people faster and faster still, with as little delay as possible.

Today when you want to read the latest bestseller, you get out your computer tablet and, with just a couple of clicks, the book is zapped onto your device within 30 seconds for you to start reading. No more waiting for days for the paper-and-ink version to arrive in your mail or, worse yet, needing to drive over to the public library and hope the book you want is available.

Social observers tell us that watching television and movies has "destroyed the attention spans" of children who have grown up turning on the TV every day. Everything on television is quick, moving rapidly from scene to scene. On the nightly news, even major stories are summed up in 60 seconds or less. In TV dramas, major complex crimes or murders are always solved within an hour.

Thus, when people try to apply the Law of Attraction in their lives, many of them become easily frustrated when results do not seem to happen instantaneously. Lots of people who try manifesting what they want for first time may quickly become perplexed as to why the million dollars they were trying to conjure did not turn up in their bank account that same afternoon, or why that lottery ticket they bought was just another dud.

For example, what usually happens after the first few tries? Nothing. Therefore, this becomes "proof" for the amateur manifestor that this process doesn't work. They may even try it a couple more times or spend a week attempting to visualise that new Mercedes or luxury yacht into existence — but nothing happens.

More "proof"!

These perceived failures then lead to a reinforced belief system that says: *"Visualising whatever you want in life and getting it is sheer nonsense."*

This then becomes the belief system and the Law of Reflection dictates that you have whatever your belief system allows you to have.

However, the Law of Attraction does work and it will work for you. The key is to remember to not make fast judgements based on short-term experiments.

Give it time.

How much time? That's easy: As much time as it takes. Better yet, don't think about time at all. Life is a journey. There is no rush. Everything is happening in the NOW. It's best not to obsess over time or worry about when things might happen or when they don't happen. You just have to completely believe manifesting works – and it will.

Again, remember the Law of Reflection. This tells us that what we see around ourselves right now — including what we "have" and do "not have" — is exactly what we have been working so hard to create all along, whether we know it or not.

This is the right place to start. The Law of Reflection will tell you where you are right now. ACCEPT where you are right now and realise you are the one who created it all.

From this point of acceptance, you have a solid foundation on which to start building the kind of life you have always dreamed of enjoying. Maybe it will take time for the various aspects of your consciousness to catch up to where you want to be right now. Sometimes it takes time for the highly critical intellectual mind to catch up with the deeper, vast and unlimited subconscious mind, which does not make critical judgements every minute of the day and is not addicted to an immediate-gratification expectation system.

Sometimes the "proofs" of the new belief system you want will come slowly, one step at a time, one tiny successful *manifestation* after another. For many people, it will take a series of successful "hits" before they are willing to truly believe they can manifest the things and the kinds of life they really desire. For others, a new belief system can take hold rapidly and marvellously.

A word of caution: Again, don't think in terms of time limits or count the number of times you try to manifest specific things or situations into your own reality. There is no magic pill, formula or spell. Every person is an individual. Everyone will have an experience unique to themselves. Remember that much of this is about feelings – and action.

Also, the actual act of visualising is a minor element in the process of manifesting. What's more important is to get to a point where you feel and act without a doubt in your mind that you already have what you perceive is missing. If you feel it, it will be there. If you act as if you already have what you want and it is "alive and existent in the Universe", the Law of Reflection will make it so in your reality.

Life is not a race. It's a journey. If you spend a lot of time trying to visualise what you don't have right now – you will be visualising what you **don't have.**

It's better to act as if you already have what you want and behave as if you are content in the moment. Feel gratitude for the very situation you are in right now! Feel confident that what you truly want will come into your life at just the right moment, exactly when you are ready for it.

The fact is that there is never really anything missing in one's life. You have everything that's necessary right now. Everything is always perfect.

If you still persistently perceive that something is sorely missing in your life, you can learn to accept that this is not the case. You can come to know and accept that this thing you want is not really missing; everything that completes your existence is with you right now. Have confidence that whatever you need will be there when it is right for it to be there for you.

Your dreams exist within the field of infinite possibility and you are the one who puts power into them. You do it with feelings and actions. You can shed all doubt, knowing that what you need is right there for you, right now. If you can imagine it to be real, it will be real. If you imagine it with feeling, then act on those feelings, absolutely nothing can stop you from achieving exactly what you want.

Remember that there is both a force of attraction and a force of repulsion. When you doubt something can happen, you repulse that something. If you don't feel you deserve something, those undeserving feelings will naturally repulse what you think you do not deserve.

On the other hand, if you feel completely worthy of gaining that which you want, you send out an attractive force to make it come to you. If you feel happy and joyful with the knowing that you will acquire what you want, you magnetise what you want to you – and time itself ceases to become an important factor. When you act as if you already have what you want, you marshal major forces of influence that will make it a reality.

The wisdom that is inside you right now has all the answers you need.

Your soul wants you to be happy and to live the life of your dreams. Your soul is constantly sending messages to you, telling you what to do, where to put your energy and how to recognise all the blessings that surround you at all times. Start listening!

The pesky mind, or ego self, tends to have another agenda. It is concerned with surface desires and the agony of what it perceives it does not have, of what is lacking. It tries to compensate by generating fear, hoping that fear will motivate you to "try harder", to manipulate, take desperate measures or to beg to get what it is you perceive you are lacking.

It does not matter how big or small your dream is, it will be right for you.

Don't discount anything. Discounting is repulsive. Always be in the attractive mode. Knowing you will always get what you want is attractive, no matter how big or small. Believe it! Feel it! Trust it! Always take action!

Fundamentally, we live in a world of illusion. That which we think of as real is not really 'real'. Think of the way a dream feels completely real while you are in that dream. When you dream, you are the one who is creating the total dream environment. When you wake up, you might think: "Wow! That dream seemed so real!" But where is it now? It's gone; vanished like so much smoke. It seems it wasn't so real after all.

The situation of your daily waking reality works on much the same principle. What you think about in a dream can become instant reality. In much the same way, those thoughts you hold in your mind persistently (and with feeling) will be your reality while you're awake. Energy is transformed into matter.

There is no end to what you can create. For the Universe, it's easy! It has unlimited power and unlimited possibility. The Universe is infinitely abundant.

One thing is certain: Your reality will 'Reflect' your belief system no matter what it is in this Present Moment. The good news is that you create your belief system.

YOU HAVE JUST TAKEN THE FIRST STEP

So now you have read a book full of advice on how you can change your life, how to discover the life of your dreams.

You have taken a step. That's good!

However, this book won't be worth the paper it is printed on unless you TAKE ACTION to apply what you have learned in the REAL WORLD.

Remember: think of the way people read weight-loss books one after another yet they remain overweight. Reading a book about how to lose weight is not the same as doing the actual steps recommended in reality. The "Doing" part tends to be the hardest part for many people. It's always so easy to just go on to the next "feel-good" book for yet another glorified pep talk.

However, all the pep talks, books, theories and advice in the world pales in comparison to just getting up out of your comfortable chair – and comfort zone – and going out into the real world and DOING.

Take action! Starting right now, make a list of one, two or three things you can do today to start making the changes in your life that reflect the life you truly dream about. Then do them!

Change can happen faster than you can imagine. Why wait? Why not start manifesting the life of your dreams right now. If you want some extra help – I'm here for you.

Everyone needs a little help and guidance sometimes but ultimately I can't make it happen for you. Only you can change your own life. Only you have been given the key to your own Inner Self.

So why not put the key in the slot and give it a turn?

I can take you by the hand and guide you. I can help you keep your vibration levels high – when believing and feeling and "actioning" your dreams – to help deliver you to a place that has limitless possibilities. But you just have to grasp it, feel it, apply it and do it.

A magical doorway is waiting to open before you.

.

ABOUT THE AUTHOR

ALIDA FEHILY is an international Esoteric Chaperone™. As an Esoteric Chaperone™, intuitive/psychic, author and certified facilitator, Alida has helped thousands of people around the world clarify their vision and see their future more vividly. Through her face-to-face consultations, radio talks, published articles, workshops and social media sites, Alida has managed to connect with thousands of people ready to take the next big step.

Alida guides people by helping to open their portal to the gift of self-awareness, which has dramatic effects on people's realities. By allowing people to open their minds to a new way of thinking, Alida allows her clients to find the genius within. Using her intuition, Alida helps clients eliminate the vital factors that hold them back from reaching their goals and living their dreams.

Alida was born in Toronto, Canada, and moved to Melbourne, Australia, in 1970. She was led on her destiny to query life's big questions such as "Why am I here?" and "What is life all about?" As a result she transformed her own life. Now with her amazing wisdom and knowledge she has helped lift her clients to a greater conscious awareness that has brought them abundance and success.

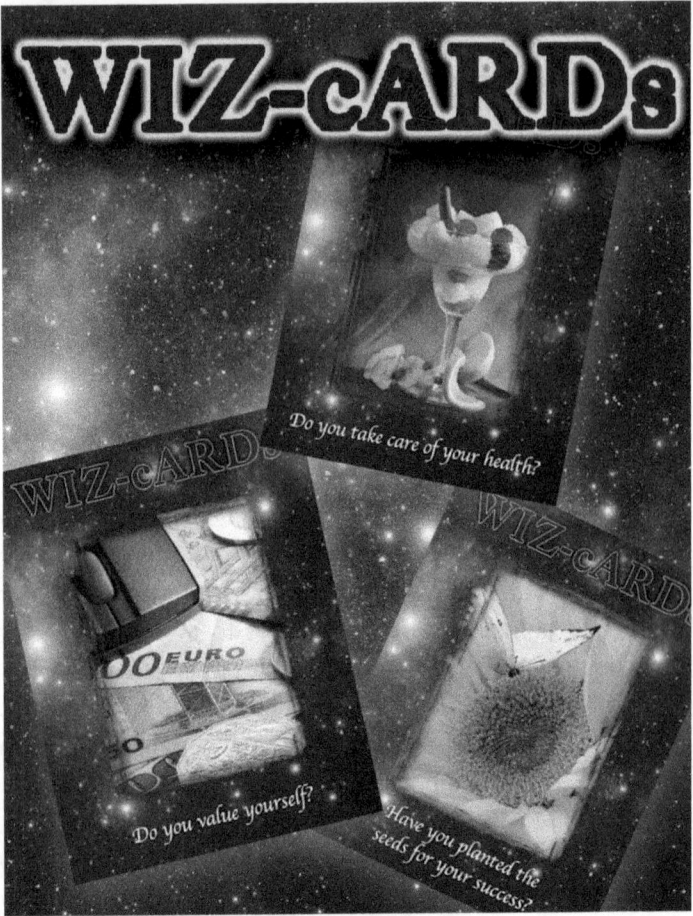

The WIZ-cARDs are your on-call mentor, providing you with questions and answers to help you uncover the positivity required to guide you forward in happiness, success and love. http://alidafehily.com/product/wizcards/

If you want a personal consultation from your friendly Esoteric Chaperone™, you can get in touch with her here: www.alidafehily.com

Free download inspirational quotes
http://alidafehily.com/quotes-social-media/

LinkedIn
http://www.linkedin.com/in/alidafehily

Twitter
http://twitter.com/alidafehily

Facebook
http://www.facebook.com/lawofattraction.psychic

Instagram
https://instagram.com/alida_fehily

(A)LIDA FEHILY

NOTES

NOTES

NOTES

www.ingramcontent.com/pod-product-compliance
Lightning Source LLC
LaVergne TN
LVHW051518080426
835509LV00017B/2097